Project Management  for

Beginners

The Practice Step-by-Step Guide from Planning and Organizing to Project Closure and Maximizing Your Team's Success

David A. Cohen

© **Copyright 2023 - All rights reserved.**

No portion of this book may be reproduced in any form without written permission from the publisher or author, except as permitted by U.S. copyright law.

Legal Notice:

This book is copyright protected. This is only for personal use. You cannot amend, distribute, sell, use, quote or paraphrase any part or the content within this book without the consent of the author.

Disclaimer Notice:

This publication is designed to provide accurate and authoritative information in regard to the subject matter covered. It is sold with the understanding that neither the author nor the publisher is engaged in rendering legal, investment, accounting or other professional services. While the publisher and author have used their best efforts in preparing this book, they make no representations or warranties with respect to the accuracy or completeness of the contents of this book and specifically disclaim any implied warranties of merchantability or fitness for a particular purpose. No warranty may be created or extended by sales representatives or written sales materials. The advice and strategies contained herein may not be suitable for your situation. You should consult with a professional when appropriate. Neither the publisher nor the author shall be liable for any loss of profit or any other commercial damages, including but not limited to special, incidental, consequential, personal, or other damages.

Table of Contents

Introduction 4

Chapter One: What's the Profit? 6

Chapter Two: The Basics of Project Planning 19

Chapter Three: Project Scope 33

Chapter Four: Building the Project Team 43

Chapter Five: Risk Management 56

Chapter Six: Quality Management 69

Chapter Seven: Effective Communication 84

Chapter Eight: Agile Project Management 101

Chapter Nine: Monitoring and Control 117

Chapter Ten: Project Closure 128

Conclusions and Recommendations 138

Introduction

The conditions of the 21st century, in which we find ourselves conducting business and solving various tasks today, are extremely changeable. To adapt, it is always necessary to find new methods and pathways for problem-solving. Project Management can be referred to as the most popular and effective tool for achieving objectives, underscoring its relevance in contemporary times.

In their operations, project management is used by companies involved in small, medium, and large-scale businesses, federal organizations, and even investment corporations, governmental authorities, and state enterprises. Project management embodies the intricate blend of planning and coordinating resources for the triumphant completion of specific project objectives and tasks. Each project represents a distinctive endeavor with a set beginning and conclusion, aiming to realize a specific result with a predetermined collection of resources.

If this book has caught your attention, it's likely that you're keen to deepen your understanding of project management. Perhaps you've found yourself suddenly in a project management role, or maybe you're just naturally intrigued by this domain. Regardless of the reason, you've landed at the right spot. This book is crafted to walk you through the fundamentals of project management, gradually introducing you to the key principles and techniques.

We'll unravel the different phases of a project lifecycle, delve into prevalent project management methodologies, investigate the significance of team dynamics, uncover aspects of risk and quality management, among other topics. Our aim is not merely to comprehend the theoretical aspects but also to grasp how to apply them practically in real-life situations.

By the conclusion of this explorative journey, you should possess a robust fundamental comprehension of project management and its essential aspects, feel self-assured in participating in project-related dialogues, and be prepared to implement what you've absorbed in real-world situations.

So, let's turn the page and embark on this way together!

Chapter One: What's the Profit?

Project management, in its most essential form, represents a systematic way of achieving objectives. This concept is part and parcel of our everyday activities, often without us even being aware of it. Whenever we strive to complete a task that demands a sequence of steps, we're engaged in a project. The process of overseeing these steps to reach the end goal efficiently is what constitutes project management.

The concept of project management takes on a different level of complexity in a professional setting. It entails the careful coordination, organization, supervision, and leadership needed to attain specific targets within set parameters of time, budget, and quality. The projects handled could range from creating innovative software, constructing infrastructure, or rolling out a marketing campaign.

What sets project management apart from the general term 'management' is its inherent time-bound characteristic. A project carries a fixed start and end point, usually dictated by the delivery of a specific result. This could be a tangible product, a service, or even a procedural enhancement.

The project manager plays a crucial role in this scenario. They're responsible for outlining the project's boundaries, determining the objectives, and overseeing the tasks and resources to achieve those objectives. Navigating potential obstacles, managing stakeholder expectations, keeping communication lines open, and ensuring the project remains within its defined budget and timeline also fall under their purview.

Project management methodologies provide a well-structured roadmap for dealing with these potential hurdles. They range from the traditional waterfall models, which emphasize sequential progress, to the more flexible and adaptable Agile techniques. These strategies give project managers a diverse set of tools to successfully shepherd projects from inception to conclusion.

Project management carries an importance that stretches far beyond just enabling businesses to complete projects in a timely manner and within the allocated budget. While these aspects are certainly important, the true essence of project management lies in its capacity to instill structure, transparency, and strategic harmony into the tasks being undertaken, thereby empowering businesses to operate at their maximum capacity.

Let's explore why project management carries such weight:

Structure and Organization: Particularly in the case of larger and more intricate projects, things can swiftly become unmanageable without a structured approach. Project management delivers a blueprint for executing project tasks, ensuring that nothing slips through the cracks and that all team members understand their roles. This facilitates comprehensive planning in terms of resources, time, and budget, and provides a framework within which the project must be carried out.

Risk Management: Every project is subject to risks. These risks can influence the project's timeline, budget, quality, and even its overall viability. Project management includes the systematic process of identifying, evaluating, and developing strategies to deal with these possible threats. Taking a proactive stance on risk can help prevent minor challenges from spiraling into major complications.

Quality Control: Achieving project objectives isn't just about adhering to timelines and budgets, but also about upholding the expected quality standards. Project management ensures that appropriate measures are in place to scrutinize and regulate the quality of work, leading to a product or service that satisfies customer expectations and meets the project's objectives.

Effective Communication: A project brings together various stakeholders, such as team members, management, clients, and suppliers. Transparent communication among all these parties is crucial to ensure everyone is on the same page about the project's aims, status, and any issues that crop up. Project management lays down communication norms, ensuring that everyone has access to necessary information in a timely and efficient way.

Strategic Alignment: Projects do not exist in a vacuum, detached from the larger organizational strategy. On the contrary, they should mesh with and support wider business objectives. Project management plays a key role in ensuring this synchronization, linking project aims with

Impact framework:
1) What are we aiming to achieve? — Short
2) How will we measure this?
3) What does success look like? — Long term goals

strategic goals, and offering a clear picture of how the project fuels the organization's mission and vision.

The Role of a Project Manager

A project manager can be compared to a maestro of an orchestra, guiding an assorted group of individuals possessing specialized skills to unite their talents and create a harmonious masterpiece. In much the same vein, a project manager's function centers around organization, communication, troubleshooting, and leadership.

Here's an overview of the primary facets of a project manager's role:

Project Design: The planning stage is a comprehensive and meticulous task orchestrated by the project manager that sets the groundwork for the project. It begins with the project manager delineating the project scope, which sets the parameters and defines what the project aims to achieve and what it does not. Concurrently, the manager also sets forth objectives that are specific, measurable, achievable, relevant, and time-sensitive, which act as the compass for the project's journey. The expected outcomes, which can be tangible or intangible goods or services to be delivered to the client, are also defined with precision. Key Performance Indicators (KPIs) are instituted, which will serve as the barometer for the project's success. The manager identifies and compiles the resources needed for the project, such as human resources, equipment, and materials, and then constructs the project's budget based on these prerequisites. A timeline for the project is established, encapsulating the initiation, planning,

⊢—⊢—⊢—⊣ timeline

execution, monitoring, and closure phases. The project's layout is structured, segmented into individual tasks and milestones, each assigned a deadline to facilitate the project's progression.

Resource Coordination and Management: The task of coordinating and managing resources is a crucial component of the project manager's function, ensuring optimal utilization of available resources. The manager delegates responsibilities to team members based on their competencies, availability, and task necessities, ensuring that the workload is evenly and effectively distributed. The manager is also entrusted with overseeing the application of physical resources like equipment and materials, guaranteeing they are procured, maintained, and deployed efficiently. Financial assets also form a crucial part of the project that the manager must handle adeptly. They need to confirm that the budget is divided suitably across the different needs of the project and utilized proficiently to circumvent needless expenses. The project schedule is another resource that falls under the manager's supervision. They need to monitor the timeline for each task, modify the schedule to accommodate shifts, and manage any complications that could impact the project's timeframe.

Communication: Communication forms the backbone of a project manager's role. The project manager serves as the hub for information exchange between various stakeholders, such as clients, executives, suppliers, team members, and any other parties with a stake in the project. The manager ensures that all stakeholders are kept abreast of the project's progression, modifications in the plan or scope, and any challenges that may have surfaced. This communication must be lucid, succinct, timely, and tailored to the audience to ensure everyone comprehends the information being relayed. This also involves orchestrating meetings, disseminating project updates and reports, and fostering a seamless interchange of information among team members and stakeholders.

Problem Solving: When obstacles or challenges surface in a project, the project manager often stands as the primary bulwark against these issues. The manager needs to be skilled at spotting these hitches, dissecting the root cause, and orchestrating suitable resolutions. This usually demands a strong capacity for critical thinking, analytical prowess, and decision-making capabilities. The manager also needs to exhibit flexibility and the ability to tweak the project plan to incorporate these solutions. The solutions must be designed in a way that keeps the project on course towards its targets, maintaining its timeline and budget.

Leadership: Leadership is a fundamental hallmark of a successful project manager. In the role of a leader, the project manager inspires and directs the project team, nurturing a positive, collaborative, and efficient workspace. The manager ensures the team operates cohesively towards accomplishing the project's objectives, and their leadership style must inspire team members to deliver their best performance. The project manager is also responsible for managing any discord that may occur within the team or with stakeholders, deploying conflict resolution skills to sustain harmony and cooperation. By establishing clear expectations, offering feedback, and acknowledging the contributions of team members, the project manager propels the team towards accomplishing the project's objectives.

The role of a project manager is multi-dimensional, necessitating a diverse assortment of skills. They need to be superb communicators, effective leaders, strategic thinkers, and skilled problem solvers. They should be capable of managing multiple tasks and stakeholders, making critical decisions under pressure, and adapting to changes and challenges. Above all, they must maintain the alignment of the project with its objectives and steer it towards a successful completion.

The Project Lifecycle

The project lifecycle typically includes four main phases: Initiation, Planning, Execution, and Closure. Each phase represents a different stage in the project, with different activities and deliverables. Here's a brief overview of each phase:

Initiation: The initiation stage is the inaugural step in the project lifecycle, where the project idea materializes. During the inception phase, the project's aim, scope, and objectives are pinpointed and defined. This involves understanding the project's intended outcome, the resources it will draw upon, the constraints within which it will function, and the envisaged end product or result. A practicability analysis is performed to assess the feasibility of the project, considering factors like technical practicability, financial practicability, operational

1) Initiation: design, define & consult & refine

practicability, and legal practicability. Principal stakeholders are recognized in this phase; these individuals or organizations stand to be impacted by or have a vested interest in the project. These stakeholders might comprise project sponsors, clients, end-users, project team members, and regulatory bodies. The project charter is also formulated in the inception phase. This formal document provides the green light for the project, outlining the project's objectives, scope, deliverables, and stakeholders. By the conclusion of the inception phase, the project has an unmistakably defined trajectory and formal endorsement from the organization.

Planning: The blueprinting phase of a project involves charting the course the project will navigate from commencement to conclusion. The project manager, alongside the project team, creates a detailed project management plan. This plan incorporates elements such as the project timeline, which delineates when each task or activity in the project will initiate and culminate; the budget, which provides details on the projected costs of the project; quality criteria that the project deliverables need to satisfy; the communication plan, which sets out how information will be disseminated among project stakeholders; and the risk management plan, which pinpoints potential risks and strategizes how to mitigate them. Additional auxiliary plans like procurement plan, resource management plan, or stakeholder engagement plan may also be included as required. The outcome of the blueprinting phase is an exhaustive and well-structured project management plan that will steer the project team during the implementation phase.

Execution: The implementation phase is where the actual labor of the project is performed. In this phase, the project team, under the coordination of the project manager, strives to complete the tasks defined in the project management plan to deliver the project outputs. The project manager directs the team's tasks, supervises the allocation and consumption of resources, tracks the project's progress against the plan, and frequently communicates with stakeholders to keep them updated on the project status. During the implementation phase, quality assurance procedures are deployed to ensure that the project deliverables fulfill the defined quality benchmarks. Additionally, alterations that transpire during the project are managed, and potential risks are mitigated to avert them from disrupting the project's advancement.

Closure: The closure phase signifies the official conclusion of the project. In this phase, the project manager validates that all the project work has been executed as planned, and that the project's objectives have been accomplished. The project deliverables are formally approved and transferred to the client or the assigned entity. After the handover, a post-project evaluation or lessons learned session is conducted. This involves reflecting on the project's triumphs, obstacles, and areas for enhancement, aiming to learn from the experience and augment future projects. All project documentation, including the project management plan, project reports, and other records, are compiled and archived for future consultation. This facilitates knowledge transfer and can be utilized as a precious resource when blueprinting for analogous projects in the future.

Each phase plays a critical role and requires a different set of skills and attention.

Project Management Methodologies

Just as every project is unique, so too is the approach to managing it. Over time, a variety of project management methodologies have been developed to provide a framework for managing different types of projects. These methodologies consist of specific principles, processes, and practices designed to guide project teams from project initiation through to completion.

Waterfall Methodology: The Waterfall strategy is a conventional style of project organization that requires a strict, linear progression of project phases. This model disassembles projects into a string of predetermined stages, typically encompassing initiation, analysis, design, construction, testing, implementation, and maintenance. Each stage relies on the outputs of the prior one and must be wrapped up before the subsequent stage can start. This method is particularly effective for projects where the needs, scope, and outputs are well-defined from the beginning and aren't expected to change drastically, such as construction or manufacturing projects. However, its rigidity and inability to flexibly adapt to changes or new data, as well as the late testing of the end product, are seen as drawbacks.

Agile Methodology: The Agile strategy is a cyclic and incremental methodology to project management, created as an answer to the inflexibility of the Waterfall method. Agile divides projects into manageable work units termed

> Agile → sprints (3-4 weeks).
> Scrum → daily meetings focussed on
> production & productivity.

as sprints or iterations, which usually span a few weeks. After each sprint, a usable component of the project is produced, allowing for testing, feedback, and necessary adjustments. This method emphasizes continuous enhancement, flexibility, client satisfaction, and team cooperation. It proves exceptionally useful for projects with swiftly changing or emergent requirements, such as software development.

Scrum: Scrum is a subset of Agile that stresses adaptability and productivity. Projects are split into brief iterations named sprints, generally lasting two to four weeks. Upon the completion of each sprint, a review is held to inspect the work accomplished and modify the following steps as required. Scrum promotes daily team communication through daily Scrum gatherings, and roles are distinctly outlined (comprising Product Owner, Scrum Master, and Development Team members) to encourage efficient teamwork and task distribution. This method aspires to deliver valuable products or outcomes swiftly and adapt to changes effortlessly.

Lean: The Lean strategy originated from the Toyota Production System in the manufacturing industry, focusing on delivering maximum value to the client while minimizing waste. Waste is anything that does not enhance the end customer's value, and can consist of the waste of time, resources, or talent. The Lean methodology underlines continuous improvement (Kaizen), respect for people, and long-term thinking. It's now employed in various sectors, including construction, healthcare, and software development.

PRINCE2 (Projects IN Controlled Environments): PRINCE2 is a process-focused method providing a comprehensive framework for controlling projects in a managed environment. It emphasizes the necessity for a well-structured project configuration with clearly defined roles and responsibilities. It covers a broad array of topics such as project justification, risk management, quality control, and change control, divided into seven principles, seven themes, and seven processes. PRINCE2 is extensively utilized in the UK and globally, particularly in government and private sectors where resource control is crucial.

Critical Path Method (CPM): CPM is a project planning technique used to strategize and regulate a project and to compute the minimum completion time along a sequence of activities. The critical path itself is the lengthiest chain of activities from start to end, and any postponement in any of the activities on the critical path would delay the entire project. Hence, identifying the critical path aids project managers to prioritize tasks and effectively allocate resources.

Kanban: Kanban is an Agile method that visualizes work at varying phases of a process using a Kanban board. Each work item is symbolized as a card that moves from one column (representing a stage in the process) to the next as work progresses. The Kanban method inspires teams to work on a limited number of tasks simultaneously, to minimize waste and maximize efficiency. The approach aims to deliver continuous incremental enhancements to a product or service, and it is often utilized in software development or supply chain management.

Each methodology has its strengths, weaknesses, and ideal use scenarios. The choice of methodology often depends on the nature of the project, the team's expertise, and the organizational context.

Chapter Two: The Basics of Project Planning

Planning is the phase where the project's objectives are clarified, and a detailed roadmap is developed to guide the project team from the starting point to the successful completion of the project.

Here are some reasons why project planning is so crucial:

Setting Clear Objectives: Establishing transparent goals in the project planning phase is a critical action that sets the trajectory and end results of the project. These goals, adhering to the SMART (specific, measurable, achievable, relevant, and time-bound) principle, outline the project's desired achievements by its completion. They offer a direction for the project team and steer the decision-making process throughout the project. By establishing these goals, the success of the project can be evaluated, as the final output can be juxtaposed against the defined goals to ascertain if the project has met its intended objectives. By sharing these goals with all team members and stakeholders, a shared understanding of the project's ambitions is fostered, promoting synchronization and a unified mission.

Roadmap: The project plan serves as a holistic blueprint for the project, specifying the tasks to be executed, the necessary resources, and the timeline for each task. It outlines the chain of activities, assigns duties to team members, and establishes the timeline for task completion. This blueprint acts as a guide for the project team, assisting in the comprehension of individual and group roles, responsibilities, and the order in which tasks should be executed. It directs the project's trajectory and clarifies how the project will evolve from its current state to the envisioned end state.

Efficient Resource Allocation: Correct resource utilization is pivotal for any project's success. A meticulously constructed project plan articulates the needed resources, including human resources (like skills or expertise), physical resources (such as materials or equipment), and financial resources. It outlines when and where these resources will be deployed, and how they should be divided among tasks for maximum productivity. Effective resource allocation prevents resource squandering, ensures tasks aren't delayed due to resource scarcity, and aids in maintaining the project budget and timeline.

Recognizing Risks and Problems: The planning phase also encompasses risk recognition and mitigation. Potential risks and problems that could affect the project are identified, and strategies are formulated to manage them. This may involve devising contingency plans, determining risk response strategies, and assigning resources for risk mitigation. A proactive risk management approach assists in foreseeing potential hurdles and preparing to avoid them, thus lowering the likelihood of project derailment.

Setting a Reference Point for Performance Evaluation: The project plan also functions as a performance reference point, providing a benchmark against which actual performance can be assessed. It includes the approved project schedule, budget, and scope against which project execution is monitored and regulated. Comparing the project's real progress with the planned progress allows project managers to pinpoint deviations, analyze performance trends, and enact necessary corrective actions to realign the project. This facilitates more efficient project oversight and management.

Improving Stakeholder Communication: Effective dialogue with stakeholders is crucial for a project's success, and the project plan acts as a fundamental communication instrument. It grants stakeholders a clear comprehension of the project's goals, the proposed strategy to accomplish these goals, and the progress at any particular time. By keeping stakeholders updated about the project's status and any adjustments, the project plan promotes transparency, establishes trust, fosters cooperation, and ensures alignment with the project's objectives. This boosts stakeholder involvement and heightens the probability of project success.

Project planning is about preparing for success. It sets the stage for the execution phase, where the project's outputs are produced. Without a robust project plan, a project can quickly become unmanageable, with tasks slipping through the cracks, resources wasted, risks overlooked, and stakeholders left in the dark. Therefore, time and effort invested in planning are likely to pay off many times over during the life of the project.

Elements of a Project Plan

A project plan is a comprehensive document that serves as a roadmap for the project. It outlines the approach the team will take to deliver the project's objectives, providing detailed information about the project's scope, schedule, resources, and control mechanisms. While every project is unique, there are key elements that should be included in every project plan. Here are those crucial components:

Project Goals: These objectives become the compass for all activities within the project and act as the yardstick to measure the success of the project. Articulating these goals with precision is vital as they offer direction to the project team and inform all stakeholders about the projected outcomes. These goals usually align with the broader vision of the organization, playing a pivotal role in ensuring the project matches the strategic trajectory of the organization.

Project Scope: This is a critical part of the project plan that meticulously outlines the inclusions and exclusions of the project. It encompasses the project's outputs, functionalities, features, expenses, and timeframes. The scope description must be detailed and accurate, offering clarity on project boundaries and averting scope creep—a situation where the project's requirements begin to exceed its original goals. Accurately outlining the project scope ensures a collective understanding of the project's deliverables among all involved, contributing to the ultimate success of the project.

Project Timeline: This portion illuminates the project's timeline, indicating when tasks will be executed and when outputs are projected to be completed. Typically visualized in a Gantt chart, it displays the order and duration of tasks, their dependencies, and the critical path—the string of tasks that determine the length of the project. The project timeline is instrumental in supervising and controlling the project, enabling the project manager to track progress and manage setbacks effectively.

Resources Plan: The resources scheme provides a snapshot of all resources required to execute the project—encompassing human resources (team members with their abilities and duties), physical resources (equipment and materials), and financial resources (the project budget). This part details how these resources will be assigned across tasks and managed throughout the project lifecycle, assisting in resource efficiency and avoidance of resource-related issues that could disrupt the project.

Stakeholder Analysis: This section identifies all individuals or entities that hold a stake in the project. This can range from team members and clients to suppliers, investors, and regulatory authorities. The analysis should elucidate each stakeholder's needs, expectations, degree of influence, and potential impact on the project. Understanding these aspects is vital to devising effective communication and engagement tactics, thereby ensuring stakeholder satisfaction and project success.

Risk Management Plan: This part of the scheme illustrates the process for addressing potential uncertainties that could negatively influence the project. The risk management scheme identifies possible risks, assesses their probability and impact, and then delineates strategies for managing these risks. This proactive approach empowers the project team to deal with issues efficiently if they arise, reducing the potential for delays or cost excess and boosting the project's overall success probability.

Quality Management Plan: The quality management scheme details the quality criteria that the project's deliverables must adhere to. It provides a sketch of the quality control (monitoring specific project outcomes) and quality assurance (the process of auditing the quality needs and the outcomes from quality control) processes. This scheme helps guarantee that the project's outputs meet the required standards, contributing to stakeholder satisfaction and the overall triumph of the project.

Communication Plan: This section sketches out how information will be exchanged among project stakeholders. It specifies what data will be communicated, who will disseminate it, who will receive it, the modes of communication, and the frequency of communication. A well-articulated communication scheme ensures that all stakeholders stay informed about the project's progression, modifications, and any arising concerns, promoting transparency and trust among the project team and stakeholders.

Change Management Plan: This section details the process for overseeing changes to the project. It delineates the procedures for identifying, evaluating, approving, and implementing changes to the project's scope, timeline, and budget. Having a transparent change management scheme helps maintain authority over the project, avoiding unauthorized changes that could disrupt the project's progress and ensuring that approved changes are smoothly incorporated.

Project Conclusion Plan: The project conclusion scheme details the procedures for wrapping up the project. This includes processes for accepting the final deliverables, evaluating project performance, documenting lessons learned, and releasing project resources. The conclusion scheme ensures a formal conclusion to the project, provides valuable learnings for future projects, and ensures that project resources are properly tallied and reallocated as needed.

Every component of the project plan holds a significant role in managing and controlling the project. Crafting a comprehensive project plan may be a labor-intensive process, but it is a vital step in ensuring the successful execution of the project.

Project Scheduling

Project scheduling is outlines when tasks should start and finish, how long they should take, and how they depend on each other. The output of this process is usually a project schedule, often represented as a Gantt chart. The schedule acts as a roadmap for the project, helping to coordinate tasks, manage resources, and track progress. The key steps involved in basic project scheduling:

Identify Tasks: The inaugural step in crafting a project timeline is pinpointing all the tasks necessary to meet the project's goals. This process entails fragmenting the project into smaller, manageable sub-projects or work units. This practice is termed as formulating a Work Breakdown Structure (WBS). The WBS is a tiered dissection of the project into phases, deliverables, and work packages. It forms the bedrock for project strategizing, assisting in ensuring that all crucial tasks are recognized and nothing is missed. When formulating a WBS, tasks should be outlined in a manner that they are comprehensible, manageable, and trackable.

Estimate Task Duration: Post the identification of tasks, the subsequent step is to gauge the duration of each task. Estimating task duration involves predicting the time each task will need for completion. It's paramount to generate realistic estimates based on the task's complexity, resource availability and expertise, and potential unpredictability. Techniques like the PERT (Program Evaluation and Review Technique), which takes into account the best-case, most probable, and worst-case scenarios, can assist in producing more accurate estimates. Keep in mind, overly optimistic estimates can trigger project delays and escalated costs.

Define Task Dependencies: Once tasks are demarcated and estimated, the next step is to decipher dependencies among them. Task dependencies signify the relationships in terms of sequencing. In simple terms, they dictate the sequence of task execution. The four main types of dependencies are Finish-to-Start (FS), Start-to-Start (SS), Finish-to-Finish (FF), and Start-to-Finish (SF). Comprehending these dependencies is integral to formulating an efficient schedule and averting potential bottlenecks in project execution.

Assign Resources: This step involves assigning resources to each defined task. Resources can encompass personnel (with their particular skills and expertise), machinery, materials, and even financial resources. Due consideration should be given to the availability and efficiency of each resource to avert over-allocation or underutilization. It's crucial to note that efficient resource management is a key to project success, as it can influence project expenses, duration, and overall work quality.

Create the Schedule: Once the tasks, duration, dependencies, and resources are established, you can formulate the project schedule. This involves plotting tasks on a timeline, showcasing when each task will commence and conclude, considering task duration, dependencies, and resources. A prevalent tool for representing this is a Gantt chart, which provides a visual depiction of the project timeline, showcasing the duration of tasks and their interdependencies. The Gantt chart is a potent tool that assists in project strategizing, monitoring, and controlling.

Review and Adjust: After crafting the preliminary project schedule, it's crucial to examine it with the project team and key stakeholders. This enables a thorough evaluation of the schedule, identifying any overlooked tasks or dependencies, or unrealistic time estimates. Their feedback and expertise can yield invaluable insights, leading to necessary adjustments to the project schedule. Moreover, project scheduling isn't a one-time activity; it's a dynamic process that necessitates continuous monitoring and adjustments as the project advances and as new information or changes arise. This adaptability helps ensure that the project remains on track and adapts to any changes or unforeseen challenges.

Project scheduling is an art as much as a science. While it involves techniques and tools, it also requires judgment, experience, and flexibility. As a project manager, you'll find that effective scheduling is key to keeping your projects on track and delivering on time.

Resource Allocation and Budgeting

Resource allocation and budgeting are two of the most critical components of project management. The ultimate success of your project will hinge significantly on how well these aspects are handled.

Resource Allocation

In project management, resources refer to the people, equipment, materials, and anything else that is required to carry out the project tasks. Resource allocation is about distributing these resources efficiently across various tasks in the project to ensure they are done on time and within budget. Here are the key steps in resource allocation:

Identifying Resources: The first step is to identify all the resources that are needed to complete the project. T The first step in resource administration is identifying all the assets that are vital for successful project execution. These assets could range from human resources, like the project team with their distinct skills and abilities; physical resources such as machinery, supplies, or premises; and abstract resources like software, data, or intel. This stage also involves considering the accessibility and timing of these resources in coherence with the project's schedule. The identification process should be comprehensive to prevent future resource restrictions, which could possibly cause project delays or escalate costs.

Estimating Resource Requirements: Post the identification phase, the project leader is tasked with approximating the quantity and kind of each resource required for each task. This phase is pivotal in creating an effective and realistic project blueprint. For human resources, this might mean evaluating the number of hours a team member needs to commit to a specific task, keeping their expertise level and the task's complexity in mind. For physical resources, this could involve calculating the quantity of materials required or the length of equipment usage. The objective here is to strike a perfect balance that ensures the project chores are performed efficiently without squandering resources.

Scheduling Resource Use: The third phase involves planning the utilization of resources based on their availability and the project timeline. This involves designating suitable resources to tasks and outlining when each resource will be employed, taking into account task priorities and dependencies. The outcome of this step is usually a resource itinerary or a resource calendar that presents a detailed synopsis of resource allocation throughout the project's lifespan. Effective planning aids in preventing resource clashes and ensures smooth project execution.

Supervising and Modifying Resource Assignment: Resource administration doesn't cease with planning; it's an ongoing process that necessitates regular supervision and amendments. Once the project kicks off, the project leader has to consistently supervise resource usage, comparing planned versus actual utilization. If resources are being over- or under-used, redistribution or adjustments may be essential. This proactive approach assists in identifying potential issues early and allows for more effective control over resources. It also enables the project manager to respond promptly to any changes or unexpected circumstances, such as a task taking longer than anticipated or a resource becoming unavailable, thus ensuring the project stays on track.

Budgeting

Project management expenditure planning revolves around predicting the associated costs of the project, monitoring, and managing these costs throughout the project's lifecycle. Here's a fundamental breakdown of the expenditure planning procedure:

Cost Estimation: This process involves quantifying and projecting the financial resources required to carry out a project. It requires a deep understanding of the resources necessary for the project, the quantity of each resource, and the expense each resource incurs. These resources could encompass labor (calculated by multiplying the projected work hours by the hourly wage rate), materials, equipment rentals, software licenses, travel expenditures, administrative overhead, and contingency funds for unexpected events. The objective is to offer an accurate and dependable forecast of the costs to be incurred throughout the project. Various techniques like parametric forecasting (utilizing statistical modeling), bottom-up forecasting (segmenting the project into smaller tasks and forecasting costs for each), or analogous forecasting (leveraging costs from similar past projects) can be utilized for cost forecasting.

Budget Development: After estimating all the costs, they are cumulated to formulate the overall project budget. This phase includes allocating the estimated costs to different tasks or stages of the project based on their anticipated resource usage. The budget also encompasses a contingency fund for unexpected expenditures. Budget formulation helps ensure that the project has ample funds to cover all anticipated costs and offers a financial reference point against which project performance can be evaluated. It's crucial to ensure that the budget is in harmony with the project's scope, schedule, and resource plans.

Cost Control: Once the budget is established and the project commences, cost management becomes paramount. This involves monitoring the actual costs of the project compared to the budgeted costs and managing changes to the budget as needed. This necessitates keeping a keen eye on actual expenses, evaluating whether they align with what was budgeted, identifying deviations, and understanding their causes. If costs are escalating beyond expectations, corrective measures need to be implemented to align them with the budget. This could involve altering resource usage, renegotiating contracts, or revising the project's scope.

Cost Reporting: This is a crucial part of cost management and includes communicating cost-related data to project stakeholders. It involves periodic reports on the actual costs incurred, the projected final cost, the variance between actual and budgeted costs, and the remaining budget. These reports offer stakeholders a clear view of the project's financial status and progress and can help detect potential issues early. By maintaining transparency about cost information, stakeholders can make informed decisions and necessary adjustments can be executed promptly. Regular cost reporting also helps sustain accountability and builds trust among stakeholders.

Chapter Three: Project Scope

Defining the project scope is a detailed description of what the project will deliver and outlines what is included (and equally important, what is not included) in the project. It serves as a guide, helping to manage stakeholder expectations, control the project's requirements, and avoid scope creep, which happens when the project's requirements start to increase beyond the original plan.

Identify Stakeholders: The first stage in shaping a project's scope is recognizing the participants, also known as stakeholders. Stakeholders are individuals or entities that can influence or be influenced by the outcome of the project. They can include both internal stakeholders, such as members of the project team, managers, and executives, and external stakeholders, such as clients, users, suppliers, or regulatory bodies. Their needs, expectations, and degree of influence play a significant role in guiding the project's course. Identifying stakeholders is a systematic process that can involve methods like brainstorming sessions, stakeholder analysis, studying organizational charts, or scrutinizing project documentation. The identified stakeholders are typically classified based on their interest and influence on the project.

Collect Requirements: Once the stakeholders are recognized, it's crucial to comprehend their needs and anticipations concerning the project, known as 'requirements.' The process of gathering these requirements is vital to ensure that the project's results align with stakeholder expectations. Various methods, including individual interviews, group brainstorming sessions, surveys, focus groups, workshops, and document analysis, are utilized to gather these requirements. These collected requirements should be documented, structured, and prioritized for further examination and utilization.

Define Deliverables: The project deliverables are specified based on the gathered requirements. Deliverables are the tangible or intangible results or products expected from the project. They can include a physical product, a software application, a service, or a document such as a report or a manual. Each deliverable should meet a certain requirement or group of requirements. These deliverables should be distinctly defined, measurable, and specific, ensuring they align with stakeholder expectations. Deliverables are often segmented into smaller, more manageable components in a process known as 'decomposition'.

Create a Scope Statement: The Scope Document is a pivotal document that presents a detailed description of the project's scope. It includes the project's deliverables, their specifications, and the work required to produce them. The scope document should be clear, precise, and specific, with no room for ambiguity. Besides the deliverables, it also outlines the project boundaries (what's included and what's not), constraints (limitations or restrictions), assumptions (things presumed to be true), and dependencies (how project tasks or deliverables depend on each other). The scope document provides a shared understanding of the project's scope among all stakeholders and serves as a guide for future project decisions.

Develop a Work Breakdown Structure (WBS): A Task Decomposition Framework (TDF), also known as a Work Breakdown Structure (WBS), is a crucial tool for project planning that delineates the segmentation of tasks and subtasks necessary for the project. It fragments the whole project into manageable units of work, allowing for more precise estimations of cost, distribution of resources, and scheduling. The construction of a TDF involves disassembling the major deliverables into smaller tasks until they are defined to a level that allows for management and execution. The most granular level of the TDF is often termed a "work package". It's imperative that the TDF is all-encompassing, covering all the work specified in the project scope and nothing more. This aids in preventing any work from being overlooked and ensures that no superfluous work is undertaken.

Validate the Scope: Post the development of the scope statement and the TDF, it becomes essential to affirm the scope with all relevant stakeholders. This affirmation process provides stakeholders with an opportunity to review the detailed project scope and contribute their insights. It's a pivotal step in ensuring that the defined scope aligns with the stakeholders' needs and expectations. Stakeholders can confirm that the scope statement and the TDF accurately depict the work to be accomplished, and agree upon the project boundaries, deliverables, and major milestones. Any feedback and suggestions are then assimilated, and changes are implemented accordingly.

The affirmation process helps prevent any potential misunderstanding or disagreements later during the project.

Control the Scope: Maintaining the scope is an ongoing process that spans the project's entire life cycle. It involves ensuring that all modifications to the project scope pass through a formal change control procedure. This procedure includes the documentation, evaluation, approval, or rejection of changes to the project scope. Scope maintenance is essential to prevent 'scope creep', a term referring to unregulated modifications or continuous expansion in the project's scope, often without corresponding increases in resources, time, or budget. This process aids in ensuring that the project remains on course and that the final deliverables align with the agreed-upon project scope. Effective scope maintenance requires frequent communication with stakeholders, meticulous documentation of all changes, and proactive management of potential risks and issues.

A well-defined project scope provides a solid foundation for your project. It helps keep the project focused, ensures that stakeholders share a common understanding of what the project will deliver, and provides a baseline for assessing project progress, changes, and performance.

Managing Stakeholder Expectations

Stakeholders can have a significant impact on your project, both positively and negatively, depending on how well their expectations are managed. Stakeholders can be anyone who has an interest in the project or is affected by its outcomes, such as clients, team members, suppliers, and more.

Determine Your Stakeholder Pool: The initial step in effective stakeholder management is to pinpoint your stakeholders. Stakeholders can include any party with a vested interest in the project, either directly or indirectly. This might encompass clients, suppliers, project team members, executives, governing bodies, or community groups. Stakeholders can either be influenced by the project's results or can wield influence over its outcome. A frequent method for identifying stakeholders is through ideation sessions with the project team, creating a comprehensive list of all potential stakeholders. This list is then structured into a stakeholder register, capturing crucial details such as stakeholder roles, contact information, their degree of interest and power in the project, along with their preferred methods of communication.

Understand Stakeholder Expectations: Grasping the aspirations of stakeholders is paramount to managing stakeholder relationships and guaranteeing project success. This requires interacting with stakeholders via meetings, interviews, questionnaires, or workshops to discover their requirements, concerns, and anticipated outcomes from the project. It's vital to recognize that stakeholder aspirations might vary and possibly clash, making this phase a crucial aspect of managing project risks. By comprehending stakeholder aspirations, the project team can more effectively manage these expectations and devise a project plan that satisfies stakeholder requirements.

Outline and Broadcast the Project Scope: A concise and well-outlined project scope is essential for setting precise stakeholder expectations. It delimits the boundaries of the project, specifying what will and what will not be encompassed in the project deliverables. It's vital to involve stakeholders in delineating the project scope to ensure it aligns with their expectations. After defining the project scope, it should be communicated lucidly to all stakeholders to ensure everyone shares a common understanding of the project deliverables. This open communication can prevent misinterpretations and unrealistic expectations, which could result in dissatisfaction and conflict later.

Develop a Communication Strategy: A communication strategy is a blueprint that delineates how project information will be disseminated to stakeholders. It includes specifics such as who requires which information, the timing of the information, the delivery mode, and the party responsible for providing it. The communication strategy should be tailored to cater to the needs and preferences of each stakeholder or stakeholder group. Regular, transparent communication with stakeholders aids in keeping them informed about the project's progress, allows for early detection and resolution of problems, and assists in managing expectations throughout the project's lifespan. A well-implemented communication strategy can significantly boost stakeholder engagement and satisfaction.

Involve Stakeholders in Decision Making: Involving stakeholders in decision-making can be a key factor driving project success. It fosters a sense of shared ownership among stakeholders, enhancing their commitment and backing for the project. Furthermore, their unique viewpoints, insights, and proficiency can assist in formulating comprehensive and informed decisions. Techniques such as collaborative workshops, focus groups, or questionnaires can be utilized to collect stakeholder feedback. Always ensure that the decision-making process is equitable and transparent, with the logic behind pivotal decisions lucidly communicated to all stakeholders. This active involvement can increase stakeholder confidence in the project, aligning their expectations with the project's direction and outcomes.

Manage Change Effectively: Changes in projects are often inevitable due to various factors such as fluctuating market trends, resource availability, or evolving stakeholder needs. Effective change management encompasses the identification of potential changes, evaluating their influence on the project's scope, timeline, or budget, and designing suitable response strategies. If a change is sanctioned, updating the project plan and promptly communicating the change and its implications to all stakeholders is crucial. Stakeholders should comprehend why the change is required, its impact on the project, and how it synchronizes with the project's goals. This transparency can help manage stakeholder expectations, decrease resistance to change, and preserve stakeholder trust and backing throughout the project's duration.

Deliver on Promises: Failure to meet obligations can swiftly erode stakeholder trust and satisfaction. Thus, consistently fulfilling your promises, whether it's meeting deadlines, sticking to quality norms, or maintaining budget, is critical. Prior to making any commitment, verify its feasibility and attainability, taking into account the project's resources, constraints, and uncertainties. If unexpected circumstances prevent you from honoring a commitment, it's essential to communicate this to stakeholders at the earliest opportunity. Explain the situation, its implications for the project, and the measures being taken to rectify it. This preemptive communication can afford stakeholders sufficient time to adjust their expectations, minimize disappointment, and sustain their trust in the project management team. Being proactive, transparent, and communicative can go a long way toward keeping stakeholders satisfied and ensuring your project's success.

More Techniques for Scope Management

Requirements Collection and Analysis: Grasping the project's necessities is a critical first step towards managing its scope effectively. During the requirements gathering stage, project coordinators and their teams assemble data from all stakeholders about their anticipations for the project's results. This process could incorporate brainstorming sessions, individual interviews, group deliberations, workshops, and questionnaires to compile a thorough and accurate list of requirements. Once gathered, these requirements need to be scrutinized for their viability, relevance, and priority. A requirements traceability matrix could prove beneficial at this point, tracing the source of each requirement, its implementation status, and its congruity with the project's goals, ensuring no requirement is neglected or implemented incorrectly.

Scope Verification: Verifying the scope involves formalizing acceptance of the project's scope by the stakeholders. It ensures that the project's deliverables are completed to the stakeholders' satisfaction and are in harmony with the outlined scope. Techniques for scope verification might include conducting reviews, walkthroughs, inspections, and tests. These methods help affirm that all deliverables are produced as anticipated and meet the specified quality standards. Any discrepancies should be promptly resolved to guarantee stakeholder satisfaction and project success.

Scope Control: Scope control is an integral component of scope management. It includes continuous supervision of the project's status and management of any alterations to the scope. A well-structured change control process is a pivotal part of scope control. This process should contain steps for documenting change requests, analyzing their influence on the project's scope, timeline, and budget, determining whether to approve them, and if approved, updating the project plan and scope statement accordingly. The change control process ensures changes are handled systematically and transparently, avoiding scope creep and keeping the project on course.

Variance Analysis: Variance analysis is a methodology used to detect discrepancies between the intended scope and the actual work executed. If the actual work deviates significantly from the plan, these variances require investigation to understand their origins. For instance, they could be due to alterations in requirements, availability of resources, or estimation inaccuracies. Variance analysis assists project managers in identifying problems early, implementing corrective actions if necessary, and making more accurate predictions and plans in the future.

Scope Reporting: Scope reporting involves communicating the project's scope status to stakeholders. This includes information about the project's adherence to its defined scope, any alterations made to the scope, their justifications, and their influence on the project. Regular scope reporting helps keep stakeholders informed about the project's progress, manages their expectations, and ensures transparency. It can also offer valuable insights for decision-making, risk management, and continuous project improvement.

By using these techniques, you can ensure that your project stays on track, delivers what it was meant to deliver, and keeps stakeholders satisfied. Good scope management is not about preventing changes but about managing them in a controlled way that aligns with the project's objectives.

Chapter Four: Building the Project Team

The importance of a project team in achieving project success cannot be overstated. A well-functioning team can be the difference between project success and failure.

A diversified project team brings together an array of distinct skills, proficiencies, and experiences, establishing a comprehensive resource base for the project. Colleagues from varying backgrounds and viewpoints can stimulate innovative thoughts, devise imaginative resolutions to challenges, and enhance the overall quality of the project outcomes. Each individual can concentrate on a specific segment of the project where their talents are most effectively employed. This optimization of personal strengths can elevate the team's productivity and the project's triumph.

The communal nature of a project team culminates in a shared accountability for the project's results. This sentiment of collective proprietorship can foster a profound dedication in team members, inspiring them to deliver their top performance. Moreover, the model of shared accountability diminishes reliance on a single person for the project's victory, thus providing a safeguard against potential interruptions. If a colleague encounters difficulties or is temporarily not available, others can step in to handle their duties, ensuring the project's continuity.

Improved productivity is one of the significant advantages of an efficiently coordinated team. When assignments are distributed according to individual skills and expertise, they can be accomplished more effectively and promptly. Furthermore, teamwork allows tasks to be conducted concurrently, substantially reducing the project's timeline compared to a scenario where one person undertakes all tasks.

A team setting offers a plethora of opportunities for collaborative learning. Colleagues can share their knowledge, learn from each other's experiences, and develop new competencies. This mutual learning can lead to a comprehensive understanding of different project facets and enhancement of personal capabilities. A collaborative environment also fosters a culture of constant improvement and knowledge sharing, crucial for the team's evolution and the project's success.

A diverse team offers a broad spectrum of experiences and perspectives, which can be particularly advantageous in risk mitigation. Colleagues can recognize potential risks from their unique viewpoints, helping to detect potential obstacles earlier in the process. This collective expertise also empowers the team to devise more efficient strategies to counter these risks, improving the overall robustness of the project.

The team structure offers a platform for moral support and inspiration. Achievements and milestones can be collectively celebrated, nurturing a sentiment of camaraderie and shared accomplishment. Similarly, when confronting challenges, the team can amalgamate their resources to unearth solutions, promoting resilience during tough times. This feeling of unity can significantly bolster team spirit and motivation, driving the team to exert greater efforts towards their goals.

Roles and Responsibilities within a Project Team

Project teams typically consist of a variety of roles, each with their own set of responsibilities. The complexity and size of the project usually dictate the number of roles involved.

Project Manager: Serves as the pivotal force steering the entire project. They oversee all components of the project, from its inception to its successful culmination. The project leader's principal duties encompass outlining the project's boundaries, formulating a comprehensive project scheme, and establishing the project's timeframe. They are tasked with assigning resources, managing financials, and liaising with team members to ensure tasks adhere to the schedule. The project leader also monitors the project's trajectory, identifies and counters risks, resolves predicaments emerging during the project's lifespan, and verifies that the project remains within its stipulated boundaries. Interaction is a vital aspect of the project leader's function. They maintain consistent contact with stakeholders, share updates on the project's status, and manage their anticipations.

Project Sponsor: Generally a top-tier executive within the organization, serves as the project's champion. They confer strategic orientation for the project and are accountable for its ultimate success. The project advocate allocates resources and support required for the project, takes key strategic decisions, and gives consent to significant alterations in the project's boundaries, timeline, or budget. They also play a pivotal role in endorsing the project within the organization and rectifying any organizational obstacles or conflicts the project might confront. The project advocate collaborates closely with the project leader, offering advice and support as required.

Coordinator: Assists the project leader in executing administrative and coordination tasks. Their obligations include arranging and coordinating meetings, preserving and updating project records, coordinating communication amongst team members and stakeholders, tracking project duties and milestones, and assisting in drafting project reports. The project liaison guarantees a seamless operation of the project activities and serves as a critical bridge between the project leader and the project team.

Team Members: Individuals tasked with executing the activities necessary to accomplish the project. They each have specific roles and responsibilities based on their area of expertise. Task force members are required to complete their designated tasks within the predetermined deadlines and maintain superior work quality. They actively engage in team meetings and cooperate with other task force members to attain the project objectives. If they encounter any complications or anticipate any risks, they are responsible for relaying this promptly to the project leader. Essentially, they are the driving force propelling the project towards its successful completion.

Business Analyst: The position of a business strategy interpreter is vital in grasping, scrutinizing, and translating the business prerequisites and objectives of the project. They maintain a close relationship with both stakeholders and the project workforce to ensure that the anticipations and necessities are correctly deciphered and incorporated into the project's blueprint. Business strategy interpreters foster communication, confirming that the prerequisites are distinct, quantifiable, and synchronized with the business plan. They are typically assigned the task of creating comprehensive business interpretation documents, which demarcate and sketch the business necessities, procedures, and data essential for the successful execution of the project.

Quality Assurance Specialist: The Quality Assurance (QA) Expert is charged with confirming that the project's output adheres to the mandatory quality norms and aligns with the project aims. They implement quality monitoring mechanisms, conduct regular quality assessments on the project outcomes, and document the results. Their role entails defining quality parameters, setting up procedures for quality oversight, pinpointing quality issues, and suggesting enhancements. The QC expert ensures that any flaws or discrepancies are detected early, and the required remedial measures are taken. Essentially, they strive to minimize mistakes, decrease redoing tasks, and guarantee that the final product or service meets the anticipated standards and gratifies the stakeholders.

Risk Manager: Plays a crucial role in the project crew by recognizing potential risks that could negatively influence the project. They carry out risk evaluations to measure the severity and likelihood of risks and devise risk management strategies to neutralize these risks. Their role encompasses recording risks, applying risk mitigation tactics, and regularly reassessing and updating the risk log. They convey information about potential risks and their mitigation plans to the project crew and stakeholders, enabling them to make well-informed decisions and to be ready for any unfavorable events that might occur.

Stakeholders: Although not part of the primary project crew, are essential to the project's achievement. They are individuals, groups, or organizations with a vested interest in the project or those who may be impacted by the project's result. Interest holders can comprise clients, end-users, project advocates, employees, or regulatory entities. Their responsibilities fluctuate based on their association with the project but may involve providing insights during the planning phase, contributing to crucial decision-making processes, backing the project's implementation, and authenticating deliverables. Engagement with interest holders is crucial throughout the project lifecycle, as their backing can significantly influence the project's triumph or downfall.

Techniques for Team Building and Motivation

Creating a cohesive and motivated team is a crucial element in the triumph of a project.. Team building enhances communication, collaboration, and overall productivity. It nurtures the relationships among team members and promotes a positive working environment. Similarly, motivation ensures that team members are enthusiastic, engaged, and committed to the project's goals.

Defining Precise Objectives: A lucid and collective comprehension of the goals the team is striving towards can act as a strong source of inspiration. Clearly articulate the project's targets and ensure each group member comprehends their part in accomplishing these.

Open and Transparent Communication: Communication is the cornerstone of any prosperous team. Honest and unambiguous interaction promotes the uninhibited exchange of ideas, encourages cooperation, and assists in resolving disputes promptly. It encourages a culture of trust and mutual respect, where group members feel appreciated and heard. This can be facilitated through routine meetings, feedback discussions, and open-door practices where group members feel at ease expressing their opinions and concerns. The use of cooperative tools and platforms can also aid in maintaining effective interaction, especially in remote or dispersed teams.

Recognize and Reward Achievements: Acknowledging and appreciating the group members' diligent work and accomplishments is a potent motivation enhancer. This can be achieved through public recognition during group meetings, performance awards, or symbols of appreciation. Recognition helps make group members feel valued and acknowledged for their contributions, which can boost morale and increase motivation. Rewards don't always have to be monetary; personalized thank-you notes, extra leave, or professional growth opportunities can also act as effective rewards.

Team Building Activities: Group building exercises are an excellent method to improve group cohesion, cultivate trust, and encourage a sense of camaraderie. These exercises can range from collaborative problem-solving tasks, workshops, and training sessions to more casual and social events like group outings, shared meals, or enjoyable office games. Group building exercises can assist group members in understanding each other's strengths, weaknesses, and working styles better. This understanding can enhance collaboration, boost group spirit, and ultimately improve group performance. A group that takes pleasure in working together is more likely to stay driven and committed to achieving their mutual goals.

Provide Opportunities for Growth and Development: Facilitating individual advancement and progress can act as a potent inspirational element for team members. This can be realized by offering chances for learning and progress such as workshops, training programs, conferences, or even mentorship initiatives. You can also allocate demanding tasks that necessitate team members to extend their competencies and acquire new abilities. Such opportunities demonstrate that the organization values their personal and professional evolution, leading to elevated job fulfillment and motivation. It's crucial to harmonize these opportunities with the individual's career aspirations and interests to optimize their effectiveness.

Empower Team Members: Enabling team members involves providing them with the authority, resources, and independence to make decisions about their work. This can encompass permitting them to set their own targets, select their working methods, or make decisions about how to resolve issues. Empowerment augments team members' sense of self-governance and control, which can lead to higher job fulfillment and motivation. It indicates faith in their abilities and judgment, which can amplify their confidence and involvement. However, empowerment should be complemented by clear communication of expectations, sufficient support, and constructive criticism to guide decision-making and performance.

Promote a Positive Work Environment: A positive work atmosphere is one where team members feel backed, appreciated, and esteemed. This can be promoted through a culture of transparent communication, cooperation, and mutual respect. Providing the necessary resources and tools for team members to execute their job effectively can also contribute to a positive work atmosphere. Flexible work policies can encourage a balanced work-life routine, while fair and transparent conflict resolution procedures can ensure that issues are handled constructively. A positive work atmosphere enhances team cohesion, job satisfaction, and motivation.

Lead by Example: As a project manager, your actions establish the standard for the team. Exuding a positive demeanor, showing commitment to the project, adhering to ethical norms, and displaying a robust work ethic can inspire your team members to follow suit. This also involves acknowledging your missteps, treating everyone with respect, and promoting a culture of learning and continuous improvement. Demonstrating leadership shows that you not only preach, but also practice the values and behaviors that you expect from your team, which can cultivate trust and inspire them to replicate these behaviors.

Managing Team Dynamics and Conflicts

In any project, team dynamics play a role in the team's overall performance and the project's success. The way team members interact, communicate, and work together is influenced by these dynamics. At the same time, conflicts are inevitable in any team setting. Managed properly, conflict can lead to better ideas and decisions. But if not handled effectively, it can lead to tension, decreased productivity, and team discord.

Given that each team member contributes unique skills, experiences, cultural nuances, and perspectives, it's crucial to acknowledge and appreciate this diversity. Comprehending the varied viewpoints within your team can stimulate more innovative problem-solving and superior decision-making, as it benefits from a broader spectrum of ideas and insights. Furthermore, demonstrating respect for individual variations nurtures a culture of inclusivity and acceptance, minimizing potential disagreements and misinterpretations. This can encompass endorsing awareness about diversity, promoting empathy and broad-mindedness, and ensuring impartial and equitable treatment of all team members.

Effective communication serves as the structural core of any successful team. Promoting an environment where team members can express their thoughts, ideas, and concerns in a transparent and candid way fosters a sense of integrity and trust within the team. In order to achieve this, it's critical to create a secure and supportive atmosphere where everyone feels at ease to speak their mind without apprehension of judgment or retaliation. Regular team assemblies, feedback sessions, and one-on-one conversations can facilitate this level of communication. Furthermore, as a project manager, you should exemplify transparent and candid dialogue by sharing information openly, admitting errors, and actively listening to others' viewpoints.

Clear standards and anticipations offer a guide for how team members should engage and cooperate. They encompass various facets such as communication protocols, decision-making procedures, task responsibilities, meeting decorum, and conflict resolution mechanisms. By establishing these guidelines at the onset of the project, you can lessen misunderstandings and ensure everyone is on the same page about how to conduct themselves within the team. It's critical to involve all team members in the process of setting these norms to secure their involvement and commitment.

Nurturing a sense of teamwork and cooperation can lead to more efficient and harmonious team operation. This involves fostering a team spirit where members are urged to collaborate towards common objectives, exchange ideas openly, and support each other in their tasks. Team building activities can be an effective way to strengthen interpersonal relationships, build trust, and enhance cooperation. These activities could range from collaborative problem-solving tasks to informal social gatherings. Additionally, recognizing and rewarding cooperative efforts can further emphasize the importance of teamwork within the team.

Disputes are an inevitable occurrence in any team due to variations in viewpoints, perspectives, or interests. However, if not promptly attended to, disputes can escalate, harming team unity and productivity. Therefore, it's essential to tackle disputes quickly and positively using different dispute resolution strategies. Mediation involves a neutral third party aiding a resolution between conflicting parties. Negotiation is a straightforward conversation between the involved parties to reach consensus. A team dialogue, in contrast, involves discussing the issue in a team gathering to acquire various perspectives and discover a shared solution. Regardless of the strategy you opt for, the objective should be to uncover the root cause of the dispute and include all parties in the process of finding a resolution that respects everyone's viewpoints and needs.

Regular and constructive feedback is a critical instrument for endorsing personal growth and enhancing team performance. Recognition of efforts and contributions elevates morale and motivates team members to continue performing their best. Concurrently, constructive feedback on issues or areas needing improvement helps individuals understand what they can enhance. It's important to ensure that feedback is specific, so the individual knows precisely what they excelled at or what they need to work on. The feedback should concentrate on behaviors or actions, not the person's character traits. Balancing positive and constructive feedback ensures that the feedback process is uplifting yet productive.

Chapter Five: Risk Management

Risks are uncertainties or potential events that could impact the project's objectives if they occur. They could affect the project's scope, schedule, cost, and quality. Understanding project risks allows the team to be prepared for potential obstacles and to respond proactively.

Types of Risks

Operational Risks: These are risks linked with the routine operations of a business entity. They could pertain to process inefficiencies, breakdowns in systems and controls, fraudulent activities, or disruptions stemming from changes in personnel. External events like shifts in the marketplace or technology can also source functional hazards.

Financial Risks: These risks are related to the fiscal composition of an enterprise, inclusive of the risk of insolvency. They can emerge from shifts in market situations, such as fluctuations in interest rates, currency exchange rates, and variations in commodity prices. Economic hazards also envelop budget surpassing estimates, inaccurate cost approximations, and unforeseen expenditures.

Strategic Risks: These are hazards impacting an entity's potential to attain its aims. They could connect to alterations in the competitive scene, transformations in customer demand, regulatory amendments, or technological advancements. Tactical hazards may also surface from decisions regarding the business entity's mission, vision, and strategic objectives.

Hazard Risks: These hazards are typically unpredictable and originate from natural catastrophes, mishaps, or other incidents that are generally beyond a business entity's control. These include fires, floods, earthquakes, or other natural disasters. Peril hazards also encompass hazards from human activities, such as accidents in the workplace, and technological hazards, such as system failures or cyberattacks.

Steps in Risk Management

Risk Identification: The process of risk identification involves identifying potential risks that could impact the project negatively. This is a crucial first step in risk management, allowing for a proactive approach to handling potential issues. Techniques employed in this phase can include:

- Brainstorming sessions with the project team can help identify potential risks based on their varied perspectives and experiences.

- Checklists, usually developed from historical data or industry best practices, can serve as a comprehensive guide to identifying potential risks in a structured way.

- Interviews with team members and stakeholders offer in-depth insights into potential risks, based on each individual's expertise and understanding of the project.

- Reviewing similar past projects can highlight recurring or common risks and offer valuable lessons learned.

- Expert judgment involves seeking input from individuals with specialized knowledge or experience relevant to the project. Their insights can help identify less apparent but potential risks.

Risk Analysis: Once risks have been identified, they should be analyzed to assess their potential impact and likelihood. This step involves:

- Qualitative analysis, which involves categorizing risks based on their impact and likelihood as high, medium, or low. This type of analysis relies on judgment and subjective assessment but provides a quick understanding of the risk landscape.

- Quantitative analysis uses numerical data and statistical methods to estimate the probability of a risk occurring and the extent of its potential impact. This analysis provides a more objective and precise view of the risks but may require more resources to implement.

Risk Prioritization: After analyzing the risks, they must be prioritized. This process determines which risks need immediate attention based on their potential impact and likelihood. Factors considered in risk prioritization usually include the risk's potential to derail the project's objectives and the resources required to manage it. Prioritization helps direct focus and resources towards the most significant threats to the project.

Risk Response Planning: After risks have been identified, analyzed, and prioritized, a risk response plan needs to be developed. This involves determining what actions will be taken for each risk, should it occur. Possible responses might include:

- Avoidance, which involves changing the project plan to eliminate the risk or to protect the project objectives from its impact.

- Mitigation, which involves reducing the likelihood or impact of the risk.

- Transference, which involves shifting the risk to a third party, typically through contracts or insurance.

- Acceptance, where the project team decides to acknowledge the risk and prepare contingency plans should the risk occur.

- Exploitation, a strategy used for positive risks (also known as opportunities), where actions are taken to ensure the opportunity is realized.

Risk Ownership: The process of assigning a "risk owner" for each identified risk is critical for effective risk management. A risk owner is an individual or group within the project team who is responsible for monitoring the risk, enforcing the risk response strategy, and communicating any changes or updates regarding the risk to the rest of the team. This responsibility ensures accountability and consistency in managing individual risks. The person chosen as the risk owner often has specific skills, knowledge, or authority that make them best equipped to handle the particular risk. The owner should be clear on their responsibilities and be provided with adequate resources to manage the risk.

Implementation of Risk Response Plan: The implementation of the risk response plan is where proactive risk management comes into play. This step puts the strategies that have been identified during risk response planning into action to address the prioritized risks. It may involve a wide range of actions, depending on the nature of the risks and the chosen response strategies. For instance:

- If the chosen strategy is risk avoidance, it may involve altering project plans, changing methodologies, or adopting new processes to entirely avoid the risk.

- If mitigation is the chosen strategy, it could mean providing additional training to team members, implementing new safety measures, or adopting new technologies to reduce the impact or likelihood of the risk.

- In case of risk transference, it may involve obtaining insurance, entering into contracts, or outsourcing certain project tasks.

- In case of risk acceptance, it could involve setting up contingency reserves (both time and cost), documenting the acceptance for future reference, or developing a contingency plan.

Risk Monitoring and Review: Risk management is not a one-time event but an ongoing process throughout the life cycle of the project. As the project progresses, new risks might emerge, or old risks may become irrelevant, requiring constant monitoring and review. This step involves:

- Regularly reviewing and updating the risk register to ensure it reflects the current reality of the project.

- Evaluating the effectiveness of risk response plans and adjusting them as necessary. This could involve changing the response strategy if it is not effectively addressing the risk or if the risk has changed.

- Tracking identified risks and monitoring for the occurrence of risk triggers, which signal that a risk is about to occur.

- Identifying new risks as the project progresses. A project's risk landscape can change as the project moves from one phase to the next, so ongoing risk identification is crucial.

Strategies for Risk Mitigation

Risk mitigation involves taking steps to reduce the potential impact or likelihood of a risk. This process doesn't entirely eliminate the risk but makes it less threatening to the project's success.

Preventive Measures: Preventive measures involve proactive strategies designed to reduce the likelihood of a risk occurring. This could involve optimizing existing procedures or creating new ones to remove potential pitfalls and obstacles. For example, regular maintenance and inspections could be performed to minimize the risk of equipment failure. Providing training is also a powerful preventive measure; by ensuring employees are well-versed in their roles and responsibilities, errors due to lack of knowledge or misunderstanding can be greatly reduced. Additionally, implementing robust quality control measures helps ensure products or services meet specific standards, thus mitigating the risk of defective products or dissatisfied customers. Such measures could include regular audits, frequent testing, and close monitoring of production processes.

Risk Allocation: Risk allocation involves assigning potential risks to the parties best able to handle them. In a project, different aspects will have different associated risks, and not all parties involved will have equal capacity or expertise to manage those risks. For instance, in a construction project, risks related to construction work could be allocated to a contractor who has more expertise, equipment, and resources to handle those risks effectively. The process of risk allocation is often formalized through contracts, where each party's responsibilities are clearly defined. This strategy not only optimizes risk management but also encourages collaboration and mutual support between different stakeholders.

Use of Technologies: Technology plays a vital role in risk management by providing tools and systems that improve efficiency and reduce the potential for human error. For instance, project management software allows for better planning, tracking, and communication, which can greatly reduce the risk of scheduling errors and miscommunications. In the context of data security, technologies such as firewalls, encryption software, and intrusion detection systems can be deployed to protect against data breaches and other cyber threats. Furthermore, technologies like artificial intelligence and machine learning are increasingly used to predict and identify potential risks, providing businesses with invaluable foresight and early warning capabilities.

Risk Reserves: Risk reserves are provisions in a project's budget or timeline that are set aside to address potential risks that may arise during the project. This could involve keeping additional funds (cost reserves) to cover unexpected expenses, or allocating extra time (schedule reserves) to accommodate unforeseen delays. Establishing risk reserves provides a buffer against uncertainties, ensuring that the project can stay on track even when risks materialize. It's important that risk reserves are estimated based on a thorough risk analysis, and are reassessed and adjusted as the project progresses and more information becomes available.

Contingency Planning: The act of creating strategies and actions to deal with potential occurrences that could have a negative effect on a project or business is known as preparing for unforeseen events. This encompasses developing secondary or tertiary plans to address possible hazards. For example, a project overseer may pinpoint alternate vendors in the event the main vendor fails to deliver materials according to schedule. Preparing for unforeseen events also entails pinpointing additional resources that could be mobilized in a crisis. These resources could span manpower, finances, machinery, or technology. Moreover, it outlines the precise measures to be enacted to lessen the impact of the risk. This could encompass distinct communication protocols, decision-making processes, and escalation procedures. Having this preparation in place, a business is better prepared to react promptly and effectively when a risky situation happens, minimizing its potential effect.

Insurance: Risk transfer is a method where an insurance corporation assumes the fiscal risk linked to specific potential losses or damages in exchange for a particular premium. This doesn't impede the risk event from taking place, but it can markedly lessen its financial effect on the project or business. Various types of insurance cater to diverse categories of risks. For instance, asset insurance covers losses due to damage or theft of physical assets, liability insurance covers legal responsibilities towards third parties, and business interruption insurance covers losses owing to disruptions in operations. By carefully assessing potential hazards and obtaining suitable insurance coverage, businesses can ensure that they are financially shielded from major risk events.

Regular Reviews and Audits: Routine checks and verification are critical for efficient risk management. They serve to identify, evaluate, and manage any potential issues before they become problematic. Regular risk checks involve assessing the ongoing risk landscape, monitoring the effectiveness of risk mitigation strategies, and identifying any new risks that have emerged. This procedure might involve verifying progress against project plans, examining financial reports, or overseeing performance indicators. Verification offers a comprehensive examination of specific areas, such as financial transactions, compliance with regulations, or the effectiveness of internal controls. By conducting routine checks and verification, organizations can ensure that their risk management processes are robust, responsive, and fit for purpose. These actions also assist in maintaining transparency and accountability within the organization.

Contingency Planning

Contingency planning ensures that there's a secondary strategy in place when unexpected events come into play or when circumstances don't follow the anticipated path. Essentially, it involves forward-thinking and situation analysis to soften the impact of unforeseen incidents. Let's go deeper into the role of backup strategy design in project administration:

Mitigating Uncertainties: All projects, irrespective of their scope or intricacy, encounter unknown factors. These could be unpredictable changes in market environments, technology malfunctions, or the abrupt shortage of resources, among other instances. Backup strategy design involves recognizing these potential disturbances and devising plans to efficiently manage them. This could involve crafting substitute plans, securing spare resources, or establishing emergency response groups. This proactive method diminishes the influence of unknown factors by ensuring well-planned responses are ready for implementation. It prevents projects from suffering excessive disruption or compromise due to unexpected events.

Ensuring Continuity: Projects generally operate on strict timelines and anticipated deliverables, and disturbances can result in missed deadlines or dissatisfied stakeholders. Backup strategy design aids in maintaining project progression in the face of such disturbances. By having alternative strategies and resources prepared, the project can continue to advance even when faced with hurdles or setbacks. This could mean having a replacement supplier if the primary one fails, or having extra personnel available to fill in case of illness or departure of key team members. By ensuring progress, backup strategy design assists in maintaining the momentum towards accomplishing project objectives, and keeps stakeholders informed and satisfied.

Reducing Panic and Hasty Decisions: When unforeseen difficulties arise during a project, there can be an instinctive urge to quickly take action to resolve them. However, this often leads to rushed decisions that might intensify the situation rather than alleviate it. Backup strategy design aids in preventing this by providing a pre-defined set of actions to take when faced with specific issues. Instead of panic and chaos, the team can quickly transition to executing the backup plan. This minimizes the potential for rash reactions and ensures that responses to problems are calculated, deliberated, and effective.

Cost and Time Management: Backup plans usually include the assignment of backup reserves, which are additional funds or time incorporated in the project budget or schedule to manage unexpected occurrences. This can assist in managing the impact of cost overruns or project postponements. For instance, if a critical piece of machinery breaks down and needs replacement, a cost reserve can cover this unexpected expenditure. Similarly, if a critical task takes longer than anticipated, a time reserve can accommodate this delay without upsetting the overall project timeline. This aspect of backup strategy design allows for better control and management of project expenses and schedules.

Building Confidence: Apart from its practical benefits, backup strategy design also assists in building confidence among project stakeholders. When stakeholders understand that potential uncertainties have been anticipated and prepared for, they can have greater trust in the project team's ability to navigate challenges and successfully deliver the project. This can result in enhanced stakeholder support and cooperation, smoother project execution, and a stronger reputation for the project team and the organization overall.

Chapter Six: Quality Management

In the domain of project management, quality is a concept with many facets, extending beyond simple distinctions of 'good' or 'bad'. It is about the extent to which a project or its outcomes conform to pre-set requirements or anticipations. In other words, it's about making sure the results of a project align with the original vision of the stakeholders. Quality, then, is not necessarily about the priciest or most premium option. It's about how well a product or service matches its intended use, while keeping in line with the project's goals. As an instance, in a building project, quality might relate to safety, functionality, and code adherence of the structures, rather than over-the-top design.

When the result of a project is of high quality, it often leads to greater satisfaction among customers or stakeholders because their requirements and expectations have been met or surpassed. Quality also helps in reducing redoing tasks and wastage as good quality deliverables need less fixes or replacements. Such efficiency can boost the overall performance of the project by conserving time and resources. High-quality work can also elevate an organization's reputation, enhancing its competitiveness and trustworthiness. On the other hand, substandard quality can result in many negative effects like customer dissatisfaction, increased costs due to reworking, project postponements, and in extreme situations, project breakdown.

Planning for quality is an essential aspect of quality management, aimed at pinpointing and setting out the quality requirements and standards for a project and its deliverables. It entails determining what 'quality' signifies for a specific project, drafting the necessary steps to attain that quality level, and recording how the project will exhibit adherence to those quality standards. This might involve specifying project output requirements, defining acceptance norms, or orchestrating quality control and assurance activities. Quality planning also assures that everyone part of the project, from team members to stakeholders, have a shared understanding and consensus on the definition of 'quality' in the context of the project. This shared understanding is crucial in making sure everyone is working towards the same standards, and it aids in managing expectations, directing project tasks, and appraising project performance.

Quality assurance (QA) is a structured method aimed at ensuring the quality requirements of a project are met. It requires the ongoing observation and assessment of the project's procedures to confirm they're functioning optimally and aligning with the stipulated quality standards. This forward-thinking strategy focuses on preventing flaws rather than uncovering them. Quality assurance is conducted through consistent reviews, audits, and the use of a variety of statistical and analytical instruments. By guaranteeing that the procedures are correctly outlined and executed, QA instills confidence that the project's quality goals will be realized, thus averting expensive revisions or mistakes in the future.

Quality control (QC), on the other hand, is the act of scrutinizing the project's deliverables to validate they conform to the set quality standards. Unlike quality assurance, which centers on the procedures, quality control zeroes in on the output - the tangible products or results of the project. This might incorporate diverse forms of examinations, inspections, reviews, or verifications. The aim is to pinpoint any inconsistencies or defects in the project deliverables. Should issues be detected, corrective measures are implemented to rectify them. These measures could vary from minor modifications to comprehensive overhauls, depending on the severity of the problem. Quality control is a vital stage in delivering a product or service that fulfills stakeholder expectations and complies with the project's quality standards.

Continuous advancement is a core tenet of quality management, emphasizing steady, incremental enhancements of the project's procedures and results. The concept is to implement regular, minor improvements over time instead of large, disruptive shifts. This could involve continuously analyzing the project's procedures, utilizing feedback from quality assurance and control activities, and pinpointing opportunities to heighten efficiency, diminish waste, or amplify outcomes. Approaches used in continuous improvement include lessons learned sessions, where project team members converse about what worked and what didn't; quality audits, which gauge the efficacy of quality management activities; and process reviews, which dissect existing procedures to discover areas for improvement. This ongoing, cyclical approach to enhancement aids in ensuring that the project and its procedures remain efficient, effective, and adaptable to evolving circumstances or new insights.

Quality Assurance and Control

Quality assurance is a preemptive measure that initiates at the inception of a project and persists throughout. It emphasizes defect prevention by assuring that the processes utilized to manage and produce the project's deliverables are operating effectively. The significant roles of quality assurance in project management comprise:

Process Optimization: Quality Assurance is primarily centered on the procedures utilized in the realization of a project's deliverables. Its objective is to guarantee that these processes are crafted and functional in a manner that reduces errors and yields the highest quality results. This generally requires a detailed inspection of each phase in a process to ascertain it is as resourceful and efficacious as feasible. Process refinement could include modifying the order of tasks, incorporating automation for specific tasks, or even eradicating superfluous stages. The target is not merely to dodge errors but to streamline operations in a manner that heightens efficiency, conserves resources, and ultimately, leads to the production of superior quality deliverables.

Continuous Improvement: A fundamental component of Quality Assurance is the doctrine of incremental enhancement. QA doesn't merely strive to preserve the quality of operations—it aspires to continually augment them. This encompasses continuous evaluation of present operations to pinpoint potential areas for enhancement.

For example, alterations to the project's procedures or work guidelines might be recommended to boost efficiency, decrease error frequencies, or amplify output quality. Incremental enhancement might also be propelled by technological progress, shifting industry norms, or feedback from team members or stakeholders. This method ensures that the project's operations remain dynamic, adaptable, and oriented towards continuously improving quality outcomes.

Compliance Verification: Quality Assurance additionally performs a crucial function in ensuring conformity with both internal and external standards, regulations, or guidelines. Compliance confirmation is the procedure of verifying that the project is consistent with these established norms and that the team is adhering to the prescribed procedures and techniques. This could encompass conducting audits or reviews, scrutinizing documentation, or observing work practices. The objective is to verify that the project is not just meeting its own internal quality goals but also adhering to industry norms, legal regulations, or best practices. This aspect of QA is essential in sustaining accountability, meeting external anticipations, and preventing regulatory issues or non-compliance penalties.

Quality Control

Quality control, conversely, is a responsive procedure that involves scrutinizing the project's deliverables to spot and rectify any defects. Quality control assumes the subsequent roles in project management:

Defect Detection: The chief goal of Quality Control (QC) is to locate and pinpoint faults in the project's deliverables prior to their arrival at the customer or end user. This predominantly involves a meticulous assessment of the product or service employing diverse techniques to ascertain it complies with the defined quality standards. For instance, in a software development project, QC may require rigorous testing of the application to detect any bugs or glitches that could impede its functionality or usability. Similarly, in a manufacturing scenario, QC might entail physical inspections of products to find any flaws, inconsistencies, or deviations from the specified design or function. The objective of fault discovery is to confirm that the final product aligns closely with the envisioned quality and is devoid of errors that could disappoint the customer or lead to product failure.

Corrective Actions: After faults have been identified through quality control procedures, remedial action is undertaken to fix these issues. The nature of these actions can vary extensively depending on the type of project and the nature of the faults. In a software project, this could involve debugging to fix identified errors. In a manufacturing process, it could mean reworking a product, replacing defective components, or even discarding defective units. Sometimes, a change request might be implemented to address a customer's feedback or to enhance a feature based on user testing. The objective of these remedial actions is not just to rectify the immediate problem but also to identify and address the root cause to prevent recurrence.

Final Verification: Quality Control also comprises a final confirmation stage, frequently known as 'validation', to assure that all the identified defects have been successfully addressed and that the project deliverables meet the established quality standards. This is a critical final step before the product or service is delivered to the customer. This could involve re-testing a software application after bugs have been fixed, or re-inspecting a product after flaws have been corrected. This final check serves as a safeguard to ensure that the deliverables now align with the project's quality expectations and are prepared for delivery or deployment. This final confirmation builds confidence that the product or service will function as anticipated when used by the end user.

Strategies for Maintaining Project Quality

Establish Clear Quality Standards: The crucial initial move in any project involves the formulation of defined quality benchmarks. These benchmarks act as reference points against which the project's deliverables are assessed. Quality, within the boundaries of a project, isn't an abstract notion but a concrete set of anticipations and prerequisites agreed upon by stakeholders. What aspects and functionalities should the project's deliverables incorporate? What constitutes the performance criteria? What are the acceptable margins for errors or faults? These benchmarks should be documented in a format that is readily accessible and understandable to all project participants. Moreover, these standards must be relayed to every person involved in the project, ensuring that everyone comprehends the expectations and works to achieve these quality goals.

Quality Planning: Quality shouldn't be a secondary consideration in project management; rather, it should be woven into the project blueprinting process right from the onset. This encompasses drafting a comprehensive quality management blueprint that sketches out how the project squad will meet the established quality benchmarks. The blueprint should furnish details on quality assurance activities (how the squad will guarantee quality in processes), quality control measures (how the squad will validate the quality of deliverables), and continuous enhancement strategies (how the squad will boost quality over time). It might also incorporate data on the tools and techniques to be employed, the obligations of squad members concerning quality, and a schedule for quality-related activities.

Incorporate Quality Assurance Processes: Quality assurance procedures are indispensable for averting faults and ensuring the consistent provision of high-quality outputs. These procedures should be woven throughout the project lifecycle, not merely at the concluding stages. Quality assurance might involve carrying out periodic audits or reviews to guarantee the project squad is adhering to the laid down procedures and working towards the project's defined quality goals. It could also involve process analysis to spot potential areas for enhancement, training sessions to bolster team competence, or regular meetings to deliberate on quality-related issues and improvements.

Use Quality Control Techniques: Quality control is about identifying faults in the project's deliverables before they get to the customer. Regular quality control checks should be carried out at varied stages of the project using suitable methods. These could comprise inspections of physical goods, testing of software applications, peer reviews of documents, or other forms of verification. Quality control also involves undertaking corrective measures when faults are detected to ensure that the final product aligns with the project's quality standards. By integrating quality control methods into the project management process, you can guarantee that the final product is suitable for its intended use and meets the expectations of stakeholders.

Continuous Improvement: A pledge to persistent enhancement is vital to preserving and escalating the quality of a project. This pledge demonstrates itself through routine and methodical analysis of the project's procedures and outcomes, seeking potential avenues for improvement. An enhancement-oriented approach might encompass "lessons learned" meetings subsequent to the fulfillment of significant project stages or after addressing complex issues. Quality audits might be undertaken to guarantee adherence to established standards and pinpoint areas for enhancement. Routine process appraisals might be conducted to ensure that the project's procedures remain streamlined and productive. Other enhancement techniques might include root cause analysis to avert recurrence of issues, or benchmarking against industry superior practices. This perpetual focus on enhancement helps escalate the quality of the project over time and contributes to the overall project triumph.

Promote a Quality Culture: Quality should not be the duty of just one individual or department. Instead, a quality ethos should be cultivated where everyone on the project team feels answerable for maintaining quality standards. This can be attained through various means. Training can arm team members with the capabilities and knowledge to produce quality work. Acknowledgement programs can reward and motivate individuals who consistently produce top-quality work. Clear communication about the importance of quality, both in terms of the project's triumph and the organization's reputation, can also help embed a quality mentality within the team.

Use of Quality Management Tools: A variety of instruments and techniques can be utilized to manage and improve quality in a project. Instruments such as control charts can aid in monitoring process variability and detecting trends or changes. Cause and effect diagrams can aid in identifying the root causes of quality problems. Pareto charts can highlight the most significant factors in a set of data, helping focus enhancement efforts where they will have the most impact. Flowcharts can aid in visualizing processes and identifying potential areas for enhancement. These instruments, among others, can provide valuable insights into the project's quality performance and guide decisions on where and how to make enhancements. They can track progress against quality objectives, helping ensure that the project remains on track to meet its quality goals.

Quality Management Tools and Techniques

Quality Management in project tasks necessitates the use of efficient methods and resources. These assist in comprehending, upholding, and enhancing the quality of the project's outputs. Below are some frequently employed strategies and tools for quality management.

Quality management in project work requires effective tools and techniques. These aid in understanding, maintaining, and improving the quality of project deliverables. Here are some of the most commonly used quality management tools and techniques:

Cause-and-Effect Diagrams (Ishikawa or Fishbone Diagrams): These visual aids, also referred to as Ishikawa or Fishbone Illustrations, are utilized to investigate and display potential origins of a specific issue or quality dilemma. The problem or matter is depicted as the 'head' of the fish, while the 'bones' that branch out represent categories of causes contributing to the problem. Each of these categories is further divided into more detailed causes. This thorough exploration assists in understanding the fundamental causes of an issue and focuses efforts on addressing them. By dealing with these root causes, the project can remove the problem and enhance quality.

Control Charts: These charts are a variety of graph used in quality control procedures to decide if a process is maintaining a state of statistical stability. The chart illustrates how a process evolves over time, with data points outlined in chronological order. Upper and lower control thresholds are also depicted on the chart, which are computed based on the inherent variability of the data. By comparing the data points to these control thresholds, the project team can detect deviations in the process that may indicate quality issues. If a data point falls outside the control thresholds, or a pattern of points suggests a non-random trend, it can indicate a need for corrective action to bring the process back to a state of control.

Flowcharts: These are diagrams that represent the steps involved in a process and the order in which they occur. Each step in the procedure is represented by a specific symbol, linked by lines and arrows that denote the flow of the procedure. Procedure maps can assist the project team in understanding a process in detail, identify potential roadblocks, unnecessary steps, or opportunities for procedure improvement, all of which can affect quality. By optimizing these procedures, the project team can boost efficiency and improve the quality of the project's outputs.

Histograms: These are a kind of bar chart that provide a visual representation of data distribution in a dataset. The data is segmented into bins or intervals, and the number of data points that fall into each bin is represented by the height of a bar. Data Distribution Bars can disclose patterns in the data, such as whether the data is normally distributed or skewed, or if there are any outliers. Understanding these patterns can aid in decision-making and in identifying potential quality issues.

Pareto Charts: A Prioritization graph is a type of illustration that contains both bars and a line graph. The individual values are displayed in descending order by bars, and the cumulative total is represented by the line. This graph is based on the Prioritization Principle, also known as the 80/20 rule, which posits that 80% of problems can be traced back to 20% of the causes. The Prioritization graph assists the project team in identifying and prioritizing the most significant factors affecting quality, enabling them to focus their improvement efforts where they will have the most effect.

Checklists: An enumeration of important or relevant activities or procedures is known as a list of key steps. This uncomplicated, but highly practical tool aids in retaining uniformity and completeness in executing a task. In relation to quality management, these key step lists can be utilized to verify that all mandatory procedures have been followed, all parts have been assessed, or all standards have been satisfied. For instance, such a list might be employed to affirm that all required examinations have been conducted on a product, or all needed paperwork has been compiled for a project phase. This method aids in avoiding mistakes or oversights, thereby assuring a more regular level of quality.

Scatter Diagrams: Plot diagrams, or scatter diagrams, are visual tools employed to display and study the correlation between two sets of data. Each mark on the plot symbolizes a data point, with its X and Y axis positions indicating its values for the two variables under comparison. By scrutinizing the pattern of points, one can ascertain if there's an association between the variables. In the domain of quality management, plot diagrams can be applied to probe potential root causes of an issue. For instance, if a product encounters a quality issue, a plot diagram might be used to inspect the relationship between production speed and error frequency.

Statistical Sampling: Random sampling is a technique utilized in quality management where a random subset is selected from a population for testing, with the findings used to infer about the entire population. In a manufacturing process, for example, a random selection of products might be drawn from a production batch and inspected for defects. The percentage of defective products in the sample would then be used to approximate the percentage of defective products in the entire batch. This approach permits a more efficient use of resources, as testing every single item in a large batch can be unfeasible or impossible.

Inspections: Surveys are investigations or assessments of a product, system, or process to guarantee it fulfills specific standards. They are vital in quality control and may involve physical examinations, measurements, or tests. For example, in a construction venture, a survey might involve inspecting the quality of materials used, the workmanship of the work executed, and compliance with design plans and safety protocols. The objective of surveys is to identify and rectify issues that do not meet the established quality standards.

Reviews: Assessments entail a comprehensive evaluation of a product, system, or process to pinpoint any problems, gaps, or opportunities for enhancement. They are typically used in quality assurance to ensure that the output meets high quality and aligns with the project's stipulations. Assessments can take numerous forms. For example, a peer assessment could involve team members evaluating each other's work, a process review might involve examining the steps in a process to identify inefficiencies, and a code review in software development would involve checking the program code for errors or improvements. By conducting regular assessments, a project team can identify potential issues early and take corrective action, thus maintaining the quality of the project's deliverables.

Chapter Seven: Effective Communication

Communication plays a vital role in the success of any project. As the one leading the project, you'll realize that a significant portion of your time is allocated to interacting with various stakeholders. This encompasses team members working on your project, those sponsoring the project, clientele, and other vital parties participating in the project. But what makes communication so indispensable in project management?

Clear and well-articulated communication is the pivot on which stakeholder alignment around project aims, schedules, assignments, and success parameters rotates. It facilitates a shared understanding and sets expectations among the project team members and other stakeholders, minimizing potential misinterpretations or misconceptions. Regular team meetings, project briefings, and exhaustive project documentation can, for instance, ensure everyone involved in the project comprehends their roles, the project's goals, and the standards they need to meet. This synchronized understanding eventually diminishes the chances of mistakes, inefficiencies, and redundancies, thereby augmenting project execution efficiency.

Communication forms the core of successful teamwork and collaboration. By facilitating the exchange of thoughts, insights, and feedback, it cultivates a culture of mutual respect and cooperation. Efficient communication avenues, such as team meetings, cooperative project management tools, or casual chat platforms, empower team members to express their opinions, worries, or innovative ideas without hesitation. This transparent dialogue nurtures a feeling of unity and inclusivity, encouraging superior problem-solving capabilities and fostering a culture of innovation.

Regular and proactive interaction with stakeholders is crucial to set expectations throughout the project lifecycle. Keeping stakeholders like project sponsors, clients, or end-users consistently updated about project developments, potential obstacles, and changes in plans helps to ensure their expectations align with the actual situation. Regular status updates, stakeholder meetings, and transparent reporting procedures can avert misunderstandings, alleviate dissatisfaction, and preserve trust in the project management process.

Open, transparent, and frequent communication significantly contributes to effective risk management in a project. It motivates team members and stakeholders to voice their worries, share potential risks, or report issues as soon as they arise. Regular team meetings, risk review sessions, or open-door policies can create an environment where risks and issues can be openly discussed and addressed promptly. Early identification of risks allows for timely problem-solving and preventive actions, avoiding further complications or negative impacts on the project.

Effective communication is the cornerstone to fostering a positive and motivating project environment. Recognizing team members' efforts, celebrating milestones, and keeping everyone informed about project progress can boost morale and engagement. Regular updates, personal acknowledgments, team-building activities, or recognition events can foster a sense of belonging and appreciation, leading to higher productivity, quality of work, and overall project success.

Communication also acts as a critical channel for the flow of crucial information, guaranteeing that decisions are driven by accurate, current, and all-inclusive information. Whether it involves sharing updates, circulating research results, or gathering feedback from team members or stakeholders, communication enables decisions to be well-informed. It makes certain that the project leader and the team possess knowledge of the project's condition, risks, resources, and opportunities prior to making vital decisions. Moreover, communication aids in achieving consensus or support from team members and stakeholders affected by these decisions. Thus, effective communication minimizes the chances of uninformed decisions that could hamper the project's advancement or quality.

Interaction establishes a necessary feedback cycle that enables project managers to continuously oversee and control project performance. By consistently interacting with team members, stakeholders, and leveraging project management tools, project managers can monitor project advancement, resource usage, and the accomplishment of milestones. If performance discrepancies, such as delays, cost overruns, or quality concerns, are identified, communication enables these issues to be promptly underscored and addressed. Regular status meetings, progress reports, or digital dashboards are some methods through which communication assists in project control. The feedback obtained through these mediums can steer necessary adjustments or corrective actions, ensuring the project stays in line with its goals and targets. Fundamentally, communication makes certain that project control is a dynamic, interactive process, not a static, one-time occurrence.

Communication Plan

Developing a comprehensive communication strategy encompasses several pivotal steps:

Identify Your Stakeholders: Identifying the stakeholders is a critical starting point in developing an effective communication strategy. In the scope of project management, stakeholders are individuals, groups, or entities that possess a vested interest or are influenced by the project's results. They can be internal constituents, such as team members, project leaders, or corporate executives, or external parties, like clients, vendors, regulatory agencies, or the general public. Gaining an understanding of your stakeholder environment is crucial as it dictates who needs to be informed about the project. This phase requires listing all potential stakeholders and scrutinizing their interests, power, and expectations related to the project. It's vital to remember that stakeholder recognition is a continuous process since stakeholders can evolve throughout the project's duration.

Define Information Needs: Upon recognizing the stakeholders, it's vital to comprehend and delineate their distinct information requirements. Various stakeholders will have different information needs based on their role, interest, and extent of involvement in the project. For example, project team members will need comprehensive, practical information, whereas top-level executives may only need summarized progress updates. Determining information requirements involves deciding what information should be disseminated, its depth, and the communication frequency. It may also include specifying the information format—whether it will be numerical (like budget reports) or descriptive (like performance feedback).

Choose Communication Methods: After the information needs are determined, the ensuing step is to pick the suitable communication modes or channels. This choice should be made considering the type of information to be distributed, the stakeholder preferences, the immediacy of the communication, and the resources at hand. Popular communication modes include emails for formal interaction, project management software for task updates, meetings for collective discussions and decision-making, and phone calls or instant messages for swift, informal communication. The objective should be to guarantee clear, prompt, and efficient communication.

Set Communication Timelines: Forming a communication timetable is the concluding step in crafting a project communication strategy. This requires deciding when (the hour of the day) and how frequently (the frequency) each kind of communication will take place. The schedule could be based on time intervals—daily, weekly, monthly, and so on, or linked to project milestones or phases. Regular, constant communication helps to keep stakeholders apprised, encourages transparency, and enables timely detection and resolution of any issues. It's crucial to find a balance in setting communication schedules to ensure stakeholders are well-informed but not swamped with information.

Delegate Roles: A fundamental step in a comprehensive communication strategy is to distinctly define and delegate communication tasks. This ensures that all communication-associated duties are covered, providing clarity about who is accountable for what. Normally, the project manager is in charge of supervising all communication, but other team members could be delegated specific communication tasks. For instance, a project coordinator might be assigned to disseminate weekly project updates, while a technical leader might be responsible for notifying any technological hurdles or advancements. Unambiguous task delegation helps prevent confusion or communication lapses and ensures everyone comprehends their roles in the communication process.

Prepare for Feedback and Adjustments: A communication strategy should not only concentrate on information distribution but also on feedback acquisition. Open channels for stakeholders to provide feedback, pose questions, or express concerns need to be put in place. This could be made possible through various mechanisms, such as routine meetings (in-person or virtual), surveys, suggestion containers, or open-door policies. Feedback sessions could be scheduled regularly or may be conducted as needed, depending on the project's demands. Encouraging bi-directional communication ensures stakeholder involvement, brings in a range of perspectives, aids in problem resolution, and cultivates a sense of ownership among project participants.

Develop a Document Management System: Adequate management and accessibility of project documents is another critical aspect of a project communication strategy. A documentation management system lets you store, manage, and track all project-related paperwork, making it readily accessible to all stakeholders. Such a system could be as simple as a shared network drive or could involve advanced project management software. The aim is to have a centralized repository where project documents, including plans, reports, meeting minutes, change requests, and other project artifacts, are stored in a structured manner. This improves transparency, promotes collaboration, and ensures all stakeholders have the latest, most accurate information.

Review and Update the Plan: Similar to other project management processes, the communication plan should be dynamic, accommodating modifications as the project progresses. Regular assessments of the communication plan should be scheduled to ensure it continues to satisfy the project's requirements and stakeholders' expectations. These evaluations could coincide with project milestones, major project alterations, or predetermined time intervals. During each assessment, stakeholders' feedback should be considered, and the plan should be modified as needed to address any communication difficulties or new necessities. Regular modifications to the communication strategy aid in maintaining its effectiveness and relevancy throughout the project lifecycle.

Effective Communication Techniques

Efficient communication is not just about transmitting information; it's about guaranteeing that the conveyed message is comprehended, assimilated, and when necessary, acted upon. Here are a few techniques that could help enhance your communication prowess as a project manager:

Engaged Listening: Engaged listening is a communication technique that demands complete attention and interaction with the speaker. It involves attentively hearing the words uttered, grasping the details, emotions, and motivations behind them, and subsequently responding considerately. Engaged listeners avoid interruption or thinking of retorts while the speaker is still expressing. They demonstrate they are attentive by using body language, like nodding or maintaining eye contact, and they use expressions like "I understand" or "Please continue" to encourage the speaker. They also reflect on or rephrase what was said to affirm understanding and ask for elucidation if needed. Engaged listening aids in establishing comprehension, preventing miscommunication, and nurturing positive relationships.

Clarity and Conciseness: Precision in communication implies being accurate, unambiguous, and easily comprehensible. This typically involves using straightforward language and steering clear of technical jargon unless it's essential and understood by the receiver. Brevity, conversely, pertains to conveying a message in the fewest possible words without sacrificing its essence. Lengthy, complex messages can distract the audience's attention and lead to misunderstandings. By being precise and brief, you ensure your message is understood correctly and saves time for all parties involved.

Non-Verbal Communication: Body language encompasses facial expressions, body movements, gestures, eye contact, touch, and even the physical gap between communicators. For instance, crossed arms might imply defensiveness, lack of eye contact could suggest deception or unease, while a warm, relaxed smile can indicate amiability. Non-verbal signals can complement, support, or contradict verbal messages. Being mindful of your body language and reading those of others can offer valuable insights into feelings and attitudes that words alone might not express.

Open-Ended Questions: Inquiry-based questions are intended to encourage a comprehensive, significant answer utilizing the respondent's own knowledge and/or feelings. They are the opposite of yes-no questions, which can be answered with a simple "yes" or "no." For instance, rather than asking, "Did you enjoy the presentation?" (a yes-no question), you could ask, "What aspect of the presentation did you find most beneficial?" (an inquiry-based question). Inquiry-based questions ignite conversation, invite viewpoints and ideas, and promote deeper comprehension. They are a potent tool in nurturing relationships, fostering dialogue, and gathering detailed information.

Feedback: Regular response and review play a critical role in efficient communication, particularly within the project management framework. Responses should be beneficial, exact, and timely. Constructive feedback involves more than just pointing out mistakes – it offers insights and recommendations for improvement. On the other hand, positive feedback acknowledges and appreciates good performance. This motivates team members and makes them feel recognized, thereby boosting morale and efficiency. Giving feedback with respect and consideration is essential. The goal of feedback should always be to assist the person in improving, not to belittle or degrade them.

Empathy: Empathy, the capability to comprehend and resonate with others' feelings, is an essential communication attribute in project management. Demonstrating empathy acknowledges your team members' experiences and viewpoints, fostering an environment of trust and transparency. Empathy allows you to predict how others might react to a situation, improving your ability to manage disagreements and encourage team cooperation. By genuinely recognizing the difficulties your team members encounter, you can offer better support and guide them towards the project's objectives.

Effective Written: In the project management sphere, written communication can take several forms, including emails, reports, proposals, project blueprints, and minutes of meetings. Regardless of the platform, proficient written communication should be lucid, brief, and accurate. Conveying your message in an easily understandable manner is crucial. This might involve utilizing bullet points for better readability, avoiding technical terms or overly complicated language, and logically structuring your writing. Maintain a professional tone consistently and double-check your work for spelling, grammar, and punctuation errors. Ensure your communication is comprehensive, including all the necessary information and context, so the recipient doesn't have to get back to you for further questions or clarifications.

Use of Communication Technologies: With the advancement of digital technology, today's project managers have access to a broad array of communication tools that can enhance collaboration and information exchange. Project management software can streamline task allocation, tracking, and updates, ensuring all team members have real-time access to project data. Video conferencing tools enable face-to-face communication, even when team members are working remotely, enhancing clarity and personal connection. Instant messaging platforms allow for quick, casual communication, making it easier to clear up misunderstandings, share updates, or brainstorm ideas. Getting familiar with these tools and using them effectively can considerably improve project communication and team efficiency. However, it's crucial to use these technologies responsibly and considerately to avoid overwhelming team members with unnecessary messages or meetings.

Meeting Management: Meetings are an essential aspect of project communication, but if not managed properly, they can waste time and leave participants feeling frustrated.

Efficient meeting coordination starts with meticulous planning. Identify the purpose and objectives of the meeting, and create a clear agenda detailing the topics to be discussed. Circulate the agenda in advance so participants can prepare. Begin and conclude meetings on time to respect everyone's time and keep the meeting focused and productive. Encourage active participation, ensuring everyone has a chance to contribute. Summarize the key decisions and action items at the end of the meeting and follow up with written meeting minutes to ensure everyone is clear on the next steps.

Cultural Sensitivity: In the modern globalized work environment, project teams often consist of members from varied cultural backgrounds. Each culture has its communication styles, practices, and norms. For instance, some cultures might value straightforward communication, while others might favor more indirect, context-rich forms of interaction. Understanding these cultural variations can help you communicate more effectively, avoid misunderstandings, and foster an inclusive and respectful environment. Cultural sensitivity involves not just recognizing cultural differences but also showing respect and appreciation for diversity. It's about adapting your communication style when necessary, and creating an environment where everyone feels valued and heard, regardless of their cultural background.

Communication Challenges

In the course of managing a project, you will inevitably face communication challenges. These can arise from a variety of factors, including differing communication styles, language barriers, remote work environments, or misunderstandings. Let's try to solve the most common problems.

Misunderstandings: In project communication, confusion can arise from a variety of sources, such as vague directives, undefined roles, or the use of intricate technical language. These can result in mistakes, unnecessary revisions, and disputes, all of which can hamper project progression and team dynamics. To mitigate confusion, aim for clarity, simplicity, and precision in your communication. Express your expectations openly, outline tasks lucidly, and utilize plain, direct language. If necessary, leverage multiple communication methods, like oral clarifications supplemented by written guidelines. To verify understanding, implement techniques like open-ended inquiries ("Can you describe your understanding of this task?") or reiteration (asking team members to echo the information or instruction in their own terminology). These methods foster active listening and guarantee that everyone shares a common understanding.

Language and Cultural Barriers: Teams with diverse or global composition can contribute a variety of skills and viewpoints to a project but can also introduce communication hurdles. Language obstacles can cause misunderstandings, while cultural variances can affect communication manners, attitudes towards disagreements, decision-making strategies, and so forth. To navigate these hurdles, cultivate an inclusive and respectful atmosphere. Motivate team members to articulate slowly, clearly, and utilize uncomplicated language to facilitate communication. Consider availing translation or interpretation services if required. Endeavor to comprehend and respect cultural differences – this could involve acquainting yourself with distinct communication customs, being open to different perspectives, and exhibiting patience and adaptability in your interactions.

Information Overload: With the incessant stream of emails, messages, updates, and reports, data saturation can become a substantial issue. It can result in significant information getting misplaced, misinterpreted, or overlooked, and generate stress among team members. To ward off data saturation, prioritize and simplify your communication. Decide what information is crucial and who needs to be informed. Use lucid, concise language and segregate intricate information into manageable sections. Visual aids like charts, diagrams, and infographics can demystify complex information and make it simpler to comprehend. Furthermore, utilizing a centralized communication or project management platform can aid in managing information effectively.

Virtual Communication: The transition to work-from-home has made remote communication an integral part of project management. However, it presents unique difficulties. Variations in time zones can make coordinating meetings tough, technical glitches can hinder communication, and the absence of non-verbal signals can lead to confusion. To surmount these challenges, use trustworthy and easy-to-use technology tools that enable smooth communication and collaboration. Set clear rules for virtual meetings, including punctual start and end times, establishing an agenda, and delegating roles. Be considerate of time zone differences, scheduling meetings at a time that's convenient for everyone. Encourage the use of video during meetings to make up for the lack of non-verbal signals and foster a more intimate connection. Lastly, promote a culture of patience and understanding as everyone adjusts to the remote mode of communication.

Conflicts: In project management, disagreements are practically unavoidable due to differing viewpoints, objectives, or work habits among team members. If left unresolved, these disputes can impede team cohesion, dampen spirits, and slow down project progress. It's crucial to address disagreements swiftly before they intensify. Begin by pinpointing the root of the disagreement, whether it's a misinterpretation, diverse opinions, or conflicting interests. Promote transparent, candid, and respectful communication. Listen to all involved parties to grasp their perspectives and emotions. Avoid assigning fault and instead concentrate on finding a solution. Utilize problem-solving methods, negotiation, or compromise to arrive at a solution that takes into account everyone's interests. If necessary, involve an impartial third party to mediate. Bear in mind, the aim is not to 'triumph' in the argument but to attain a resolution that aids the project's objectives and fosters a positive team environment.

Lack of Engagement: Apathy can result in minimal participation in discussions, diminished innovation, and subpar performance. To nurture engagement, make sure that communication is a reciprocal process. Motivate team members to share their views, ideas, and apprehensions. Directly solicit their feedback during meetings or in private discussions. Acknowledge and appreciate their efforts to elevate their spirits and motivation. Cultivate an inclusive communication setting where all ideas carry weight and all voices are listened to. Take their feedback into account and involve them in decision-making to help them feel valued and committed to the project. Regular team-building exercises can also strengthen bonds and increase engagement.

Poorly Defined Roles and Responsibilities: If roles and duties are not lucidly defined and communicated, it can result in confusion, inefficiency, and errors. Each team member should be aware of their assignments, their deliverables, and who they're accountable to. This clarity helps avoid redundant work, overlooked tasks, and disputes over responsibilities. Use instruments like a RACI matrix (Responsible, Accountable, Consulted, Informed) to lucidly define and communicate roles and duties. Frequently revisit these definitions as the project evolves and as tasks or team structures alter. Maintain transparent communication to promptly address any questions or confusion.

Resistance to Change: Change can be distressing, and team members may oppose it due to apprehension about the unfamiliar, contentment with the current state, or worries about their capability to adjust. Reluctance can obstruct communication, generate disputes, and decelerate project progress. To handle reluctance, articulate the change clearly. Elucidate the reasons for the change, its advantages, its impact on the team, and the strategy for managing it. Tackle the 'what's in it for me' query to show team members how the change could be beneficial to them. Promote open dialogue about the change. Pay attention to their concerns, respond to their questions, and offer support to aid them in adapting. Provide training or resources as required. By effectively managing change, you can transform resistance into acceptance and cultivate a culture of adaptability and resilience.

Chapter Eight: Agile Project Management

Agile is a project management methodology that embraces flexibility, collaboration, and customer satisfaction. It was initially developed for software development projects, but its principles can be applied to various types of projects.

The Agile approach is steered by the Agile Manifesto, comprising 12 fundamental principles. The core concept underpinning these principles is to promptly and efficiently deliver value to customers, with a strong focus on adaptability, cooperation, and client satisfaction. The principles advocate for the continuous delivery of valuable software, embracing changes in requirements even late in the project's life, close and frequent interaction between business stakeholders and developers, and building projects around driven individuals, entrusting them with the task completion. They also endorse in-person conversation as the most efficient and effective mode of conveying information, sustainable development, ongoing focus on technical excellence and robust design, simplicity, self-organizing teams, and regular reflection on enhancing effectiveness. These principles act as a guiding philosophy, shaping the behaviours and mindset of the Agile team, fostering a culture of continuous learning, enhancement, and adaptation.

Agile project management employs a cyclical development approach, segmenting the project into manageable parts known as iterations or sprints. This cyclical process enables the opportunity to evaluate, learn, and adapt after each sprint, empowering the team to respond more effectively to alterations. Each sprint constitutes a complete project cycle, involving design, development, testing, and customer feedback, concluding with a potentially deliverable product increment. This approach minimizes risk, facilitates customer feedback, and allows for necessary course corrections, leading to a more polished, high-quality product.

Roles in Agile: In an Agile project, three primary roles exist - the Product Owner, the Scrum Master, and the Development Team.

- The Product Owner represents the customer's interests within the team, responsible for maximizing the product's value. They oversee the product backlog, prioritize tasks based on business value, and ensure the team's efforts align with the customer's needs and expectations.

- The Scrum Master acts as a facilitator and mentor for the Agile team, aiding them in understanding and effectively implementing Agile principles and practices. They strive to eliminate any hurdles that may obstruct the team's progress and ensure the team operates in an environment conducive to high productivity and creativity.

- The Development Team comprises professionals who execute the work to deliver the product increment each sprint. In Agile, the Development

Team is self-organizing, deciding amongst themselves the best way to accomplish their work. They operate collaboratively, utilizing their collective skills and knowledge to achieve each sprint's objectives.

This demarcation of roles within an Agile project allows for explicit lines of responsibility, nurtures a cooperative work environment, and ensures that the focus remains on delivering value to the customer.

Both Scrum and Kanban are Agile methodologies intended to boost effective project management, albeit their methodologies vary.

Scrum proceeds in iterative cycles referred to as sprints, typically stretching from two to four weeks. Every sprint kicks off with a planning session, wherein the team determines the workload to be achieved during the sprint. Daily touch-base meetings are conducted to discuss progress and tackle any hindrances. Each sprint concludes with a sprint review to showcase the finished work to stakeholders, followed by a retrospective to recognize successful practices and pinpoint areas of enhancement for the subsequent sprint. Scrum involves three crucial roles: Product Owner, Scrum Master, and Development Team.

Conversely, Kanban emphasizes visualizing the entire workflow, spanning from incoming tasks (or requests) to the finalized work. This visualization is typically accomplished through a Kanban board, containing columns that represent different phases of the workflow. Kanban strives to limit work in progress at each stage, ensuring the team avoids overcommitment and concentrates on completing tasks proficiently. Kanban does not operate in sprints but follows a continuous process, with work being drawn from the backlog as capacity permits. The team strives for ongoing improvement, frequently reviewing the process and making necessary modifications.

Agile, while beneficial, comes with its set of obstacles. The incorporation and mastery of Agile practices often demand substantial effort and dedication.

- Agile calls for a significant alteration in perspective compared to traditional waterfall methodologies. It necessitates adaptability, readiness to embrace change, and a dedication to collaboration and constant improvement. Not everyone can comfortably transition to this new mindset, and it mandates commitment from the entire team.

- Agile methodologies heavily depend on client involvement for defining requirements, offering feedback, and decision-making. However, not all clients can offer the needed level of involvement, which might pose challenges in successfully adopting Agile.

- The flexibility that Agile offers can sometimes be a double-edged sword. Persistent changes in requirements can disrupt the team's focus, leading to confusion or delays. Effectively managing changes is critical to prevent this from becoming an issue.

- Agile stresses the importance of working software over exhaustive documentation. While this bolsters efficiency, it can sometimes lead to problems if not handled properly, such as loss of knowledge when team members depart or lack of clarity for new team members. Proper, efficient documentation practices need to be upheld.

Key Principles of Agile

Agile Project Management operates under a foundational set of guidelines embodied in the Agile Manifesto. These guidelines strive to endorse a more adaptable, cooperative, and customer-centric approach to handling projects. The key principles include:

1. Customer Satisfaction Through Continuous Delivery: Agile methodology gives high importance to customer satisfaction, achieved by regularly delivering valuable and functioning software. Contrary to delivering the product as a whole after a lengthy development cycle (as seen in traditional waterfall methodologies), Agile consistently delivers smaller, functional portions of the software in brief, recurrent cycles. This enables customers to benefit from the product early on and offer feedback that can be utilized in following iterations. This constant, cyclical process aids in delivering a product that aligns closely with customer needs and expectations, resulting in increased customer satisfaction.

2. Welcoming Changing Requirements: Changing requirements during later stages of development are generally deemed harmful to the project's success in conventional project management, potentially leading to significant rework, delays, and cost overruns. Agile, however, adopts a different stance. It views changing requirements as an opportunity rather than an obstacle. Given Agile operates in brief iterations, there is scope to accommodate changes without dramatic effects on the project's overall timeline or budget. This adaptability allows Agile teams to adjust to the customer's evolving needs and deliver a product that offers the maximum value.

3. Delivering Working Software Frequently: The primary measure of progress in Agile is the delivery of functioning software. Instead of focusing on documentation, plans, or adhering to schedules, Agile highlights the production of tangible, usable outputs. This method allows stakeholders to see and interact with the product frequently and early on, providing a clear representation of the project's progress and offering them a chance to provide feedback, identify issues, and propose enhancements. Regularly delivering functioning software, preferably in a short timescale, maintains the project's momentum and ensures stakeholder engagement and satisfaction.

4. Collaboration Between Business People and Developers: Agile acknowledges the importance of cooperation between business stakeholders and developers. It advocates for close, daily collaboration between these two groups. This approach ensures developers understand the business objectives and customer needs, enabling them to make more informed decisions about the product's development. It also helps business stakeholders stay current with development progress, challenges, and successes, ensuring the product remains in line with business objectives and customer needs.

5. Building Projects Around Motivated Individuals: Agile has faith in the power of driven individuals and their impact on project success. Rather than relying heavily on processes or tools, Agile focuses on people. It suggests providing a supportive and trusting environment where individuals are motivated to perform their best work. Trusting the team to get the work done and giving them the autonomy to decide how the work is done fosters a sense of ownership, enhances team morale, and boosts productivity.

6. Face-to-Face Conversation: Agile emphasizes the importance of face-to-face communication as the most effective way of sharing information within a development team. Face-to-face interactions promote understanding, collaboration, and swift problem-solving. When team members are located in different locations and face-to-face communication isn't feasible, Agile encourages the use of the most efficient means of communication available, such as video conferencing or chat platforms. The aim is to maintain open, clear, and frequent communication to ensure everyone stays aligned and informed.

7. Working Software as the Primary Measure of Progress: Agile puts a higher weight on the provision of functional software as the core indicator of progress. This contrasts traditional project management methodologies that might view a finalized stage of the project as progress. Agile views tangible, operational software as the testament of advancement. This focus spurs teams to consistently generate value, ensures that they stay customer-focused, and renders progress perceptible to all stakeholders. It's a transition from document or plan-centric measures of success to one that appreciates functioning results.

8. Maintaining a Sustainable Work Pace: One of the pivotal principles of Agile is sustainability. Agile advocates for teams to work at a rhythm that can be maintained indefinitely, without causing burnout or a drop in productivity. This means effective management of workloads, avoiding excessive work, and preserving a healthy work-life balance. By doing so, the productivity, motivation, and quality of the team's work can be preserved over an extended period. It also encourages prolonged engagement of stakeholders, sponsors, and users.

9. Pursuing Technical Excellence and Good Design: Agile acknowledges the importance of technical excellence and commendable design. It inspires teams to aim for superior standards in their work and to constantly enhance their technical skills. Admirable design and technical excellence lead to more maintainable, scalable, and efficient products. They also augment the agility of the team, empowering them to respond more swiftly and effectively to changes.

10. Simplicity—The Art of Maximizing the Amount of Work Not Done: In Agile, simplicity holds a high value—it's about maximizing the amount of work not done. This principle is about concentrating on what's necessary to deliver value to the customer and avoiding work that doesn't contribute to that value. It encourages teams to eliminate unnecessary features, streamline processes, and eradicate waste. This focus on simplicity results in more efficient resource utilization, quicker delivery, and a product that's simpler to use and maintain.

11. Self-Organizing Teams: Agile favors self-organizing teams as it believes that the best architectures, requirements, and designs emerge from self-organizing teams. These teams are empowered to make decisions about their work methodology, which promotes ownership, engagement, and innovation. Self-organization allows the team to adapt swiftly to changes and to continuously enhance their work methods based on their experiences and learnings.

12. Reflecting on How to Become More Effective: Agile promotes periodic reflection on team performance and processes to identify areas for enhancement. It encourages teams to allocate time to analyze their strengths, weaknesses, triumphs, and challenges, and to adapt their behavior and practices accordingly. This process of regular introspection and adaptation fosters continuous learning and improvement, assisting teams in becoming more effective over time.

Benefits and Profit

Agile project management has experienced a substantial rise in popularity over the years due to the numerous advantages it provides.

Agile methodologies are fundamentally customer-focused, prioritizing the consistent delivery of value to the customer.

This methodology encourages consistent interaction with the customer, and regular feedback cycles enable the team to gain a deeper understanding of the customer's needs and expectations. This ongoing interaction and collaboration ensure that the final product or service aligns perfectly with customer requirements and can be adjusted to meet their changing needs. Customer satisfaction is also amplified as customers witness concrete progress in the form of operational software or product increments on a regular basis. They feel more integrated into the process and have a direct influence on product development.

Agile methodologies are inherently flexible and are designed to accommodate changes. With Agile, change is not merely anticipated but is embraced, even late in the development cycle. Short planning cycles and incremental development empower Agile teams to respond to changes swiftly and efficiently, whether they pertain to changes in project scope, customer requirements, technology, or market conditions. This degree of flexibility is challenging to achieve with traditional project management methods, which often necessitate detailed upfront planning and have a limited capacity to alter direction midway.

Agile's focus on regular testing, continuous integration, and consistent reviews result in high-quality products. Defects are identified and corrected promptly, and the emphasis on technical excellence and good design culminates in robust, well-designed, and user-friendly products. The practice of sustainable development helps maintain a steady pace, avoiding rushed and potentially lower-quality work. Moreover, by constructing in increments, the team can integrate feedback into each iteration, continually refining the product over time.

Agile methodologies inherently help to mitigate many project risks. By dividing the project into smaller, manageable units, or sprints, progress can be reviewed and evaluated more frequently. This regular reassessment allows potential issues to be identified and addressed early on, which can prevent minor problems from escalating into major ones. With its iterative approach, Agile also minimizes the risk of project failure, as a functional product is delivered at the end of each sprint. The frequent deliverables also curtail financial risk by providing the opportunity to assess the project's viability and return on investment at several stages throughout its lifecycle.

Agile methodologies, with their focus on repetitive development and progressive delivery, can substantially decrease the time required to introduce a product to the market. Each sprint is designed to deliver a potentially shippable increment of the product, implying that functional features can be delivered to users faster than with conventional waterfall project management methods. This rapid and frequent delivery enables quicker user feedback and the capability to modify the product based on this feedback, ensuring the final product continues to meet user needs. Quicker market entry also offers a competitive edge and allows for a faster return on investment.

Agile methodologies cultivate a culture of transparent communication, cooperation, and shared ownership. Regular engagement among team members and stakeholders, as well as daily standup meetings, ensure everyone remains informed and that challenges are resolved promptly. Furthermore, Agile encourages self-organization, where teams have the freedom to decide the best way to accomplish their work. This autonomy results in increased ownership and responsibility, boosting motivation, and leading to a more engaged and productive team. The cross-functional nature of Agile teams also promotes knowledge exchange and learning, leading to overall team development and improved performance.

Agile's focus on iterative development and incremental delivery offers more transparency and control over project costs. Each sprint is time-bound, and work is prioritized based on its significance to the project, ensuring that the most crucial features are developed first. This approach not only optimizes resource use but also allows for more accurate cost estimation and improved financial control. It provides the opportunity to review and modify the project's scope and direction frequently, thereby managing expenses and reducing the chance of project overruns.

A key principle of Agile is the commitment to continuous improvement. Regular retrospectives - meetings where the team reviews the previous sprint - play a vital role in this commitment. These meetings offer the team a chance to discuss what went well, what didn't, and how they can improve in the next sprint. This ongoing cycle of reflection and adjustment allows the team to continually improve their processes, tools, relationships, and their overall performance. Over time, these incremental improvements can lead to significant increases in productivity, efficiency, and team satisfaction.

Comparing Agile with Traditional Project Management

Contrasting Agile project management with traditional methods like the Waterfall model can illuminate the dissimilarities and possible advantages of each strategy.

1. Classic project management methods, such as the Waterfall model, are driven by planning. They heavily rely on comprehensive upfront planning, with the project's scope, requirements, timeline, and cost being defined in detail from the outset. Alterations during the project's lifecycle are typically processed through a formal change control procedure and can be expensive and disruptive. On the contrary, Agile methods are more adaptable and flexible. Even though planning is involved, Agile methods understand that it's impossible to predict every aspect in advance, particularly for complex projects. Agile projects are iterative, implying that they plan for a short span, execute, review, learn, and then strategize for the next phase based on the newly acquired knowledge. This adaptability enables Agile teams to better adjust to changes, whether they arise from shifting customer needs, market conditions, or project challenges.

2. Traditional project management strategies follow a sequential delivery approach - requirements are collected, design is finalized, coding is conducted, testing is carried out, and then the final product is delivered. The complete

product isn't seen until the project's conclusion, which could be several months or even years after the initiation. In contrast, Agile adopts an incremental approach. The project is divided into small, manageable units (iterations or sprints), and each sprint intends to deliver a potentially shippable increment of the product. This approach implies that value is delivered to the customer regularly throughout the project, not just at its conclusion. It also allows for early feedback and the ability to adjust the product as needed based on this feedback.

3. In project management, customer participation is typically restricted to certain stages, such as during the collection of requirements at the project's start and acceptance testing at the project's end. This can create a gap between customer expectations and the final product. However, Agile methods emphasize continuous customer or user participation throughout the development process. Customers often form part of the Agile team and are involved in prioritizing features, reviewing progress, and providing feedback at the end of each sprint. This close collaboration ensures that the development work stays aligned with the customer's needs and expectations.

4. Project management methods often employ a hierarchical structure, with a project manager supervising the work and making key decisions. Roles and responsibilities are explicitly defined, and team members may operate in isolation, focusing on their particular tasks. In contrast, Agile methods encourage a more egalitarian and collaborative team structure. Agile teams are self-organizing, meaning the team members decide the best

way to execute their work, rather than being instructed by others outside the team. Responsibilities are shared, and team members often take on multiple roles, fostering a sense of shared ownership and collaboration. This type of environment can result in higher team morale, increased creativity, and superior problem-solving.

5. Conventional project management approaches usually adhere to a hierarchical format, where each member holds a specific role and set duties under the supervision of a project manager. Decision-making usually follows a top-down approach, and each team member is focused on their particular tasks or specialties. Agile, however, endorses a self-organizing, cross-functional team layout. There's no traditional project manager role in Agile. Instead, the team collectively takes on the responsibility for completing the project. Decisions are made collaboratively, often by consensus, and all team members are urged to contribute their ideas and expertise across all project areas. This flat, democratic team structure promotes improved communication, increased cooperation, and a stronger sense of ownership among team members.

6. Project management methods often place testing and quality assurance activities towards the end of the project timeline. This arrangement implies that any problems or defects are detected late in the process, which can lead to costly and time-consuming revisions. With Agile methodologies, testing and quality assurance are integrated into each project iteration. This approach means that issues can be identified and rectified as soon as they arise, thereby improving the quality of the product incrementally

and continuously. It also allows for ongoing feedback, ensuring the product aligns with customer needs and expectations at every phase.

7. Traditional project management evaluates success and control by comparing actual progress with a detailed plan, focusing on metrics like cost deviation, schedule deviation, and scope changes. While these metrics are crucial, they don't always reflect the value delivered to the customer. Agile, in contrast, employs value-driven metrics to assess success. For instance, the delivery of working software is a primary measure of progress in Agile. Other Agile metrics might include customer satisfaction, business value delivered, or the team's ability to respond to change. This shift in focus from strict adherence to a plan towards delivering value aligns the team's efforts more closely with the project's ultimate goal: to deliver a product that meets the customer's needs and provides value to the organization.

Both Agile and traditional project management have their merits and can be the right choice depending on the project's nature, the fluctuation of the requirements, the team layout, and the organization's culture. Comprehending these differences can aid organizations in selecting the most appropriate approach for their projects.

Chapter Nine: Monitoring and Control

Project monitoring and control are essential elements of the project management progression. They involve the steady tracking of project evolution to confirm that it aligns with its schedule, budget, and initial goals. Here's why project observation and administration are of prime importance:

Monitoring and control create the foundation for successful project implementation. Consistent observation of the project's advancement against the baseline plan ensures all actions are following the right path. A baseline plan is the initial project schedule, cost, and scope agreed upon at the project's inception. The processes of observation and administration involve gauging the project's performance and comparing it with this baseline. Any divergence from the plan can be promptly spotted, facilitating quick corrective actions before minor issues grow into major problems. This continual evaluation ensures the project remains on track towards its objectives and confirms that the final deliverable aligns with the predefined requirements within the stipulated time and budget.

Project observation offers valuable insights and data that drive strategic decision-making. Through regular and detailed assessment of project performance, project managers can comprehend the current state of the project, including individual task statuses, team performance, and resource utilization. They can also identify trends, like consistent time overruns for tasks, or certain resources being excessively used. This information empowers project managers and stakeholders to make informed decisions, such as if additional resources are required, if certain tasks need reprioritization, or if amendments to the project plan are necessary. Effective decision-making is crucial to the successful execution and completion of a project, and it is significantly enhanced by regular project observation and administration.

Every project contains potential risks that could adversely affect its success. Regular project observation can identify potential risks and issues at an early stage. This identification enables a proactive approach to risk management, implementing mitigation strategies or contingency plans as needed. Regular observation also allows for a reassessment of identified risks, as their probability or impact can alter as the project advances. Effective risk management is vital to prevent minor issues from growing into major problems that could derail the project.

One of the pivotal aspects of project management is assuring efficient and effective use of resources, whether they're human, technical, or financial resources. Regular project observation can provide real-time data on resource use, pinpointing areas where resources might be over- or under-utilized. This observation allows project managers to reallocate resources as necessary, making sure each part of the project has the resources required to proceed effectively. By optimizing resource use, project managers can enhance the productivity and efficiency of the project, contributing to a successful project outcome.

The procedures involved in project monitoring and administration significantly contribute to enhancing communication among all project stakeholders. Regular updates and reports on the project's status ensure everyone is up to date about the project's evolution. These updates give a transparent overview of completed tasks, ongoing work, and pending tasks. This steady stream of information encourages transparency and accountability, and it aids in managing expectations. Moreover, it provides an avenue for promptly addressing issues or concerns. Enhanced communication promotes better cooperation among team members and stakeholders, facilitates more effective issue resolution, and helps to cultivate trust. It guarantees everyone is aligned, reducing the chances of confusion or misunderstandings that could affect the project's success.

Project control activities back quality assurance by continuously overseeing project processes and deliverables. They facilitate early detection of potential quality problems, such as divergences from the project plan or non-adherence to established standards. Early identification of quality problems means corrective measures can be executed before the problems grow. Regular analysis of quality metrics also confirms that the project's processes and outputs are consistently meeting the required quality standards. Ultimately, this ensures the final product is of a high standard and meets or surpasses the client's expectations.

This activities produce a considerable amount of data, including information on project performance, the efficiency of project processes, and the effectiveness of risk management tactics. This data is a valuable resource for learning and ongoing improvement. During the project, team members and stakeholders can use this information to identify areas for enhancement and adjust their strategies or processes as needed. Lessons gleaned from observation and controlling processes can also be documented and used for future projects. This contributes to the organization's knowledge base, enhancing its ability to handle future projects more effectively. In the long run, this learning and improvement can lead to better project outcomes, improved team performance, and elevated customer satisfaction.

Tools and techniques for effective project monitoring

Efficient project monitoring calls for suitable instruments and methodologies. These can fluctuate depending on the project's scale, intricacy, and distinct requisites. Nevertheless, the following represent some universally utilized instruments and methodologies that project administrators can employ:

Project Management Software: This type of software encompasses a set of tools constructed to assist project administrators and teams to collaborate and accomplish their objectives more proficiently. These utilities can range from straightforward to-do lists and task tracking devices to intricate, multi-functional systems that govern all aspects of project planning and implementation. They frequently offer features for task allocation, timeline establishment, resource distribution, risk administration, documentation, communication, and reporting. Some well-known examples of project management software include Microsoft Project, renowned for its robustness in project scheduling and resource administration; Asana, known for its user-friendly layout and flexible task management attributes; Trello, which utilizes a card-based system to arrange tasks and monitor progress; and Jira, a powerful utility favored by software development teams for issue tracking and managing Agile workflows. The selection of software relies on the scale, intricacy, and specific necessities of the project.

Dashboards: Dashboards are graphic interfaces that visually exhibit key project data. They compile and present information in an accessible format, usually via graphs, charts, and tables. Dashboards can monitor an array of key performance indicators, such as task completion status, budget utilization, time tracking, risk levels, and more. By presenting this data visually, dashboards permit project administrators to promptly identify trends, monitor project health, and spot any areas of concern that might require attention. Dashboards also aid in communication with stakeholders, offering a quick overview of the project's status.

Gantt Charts: Gantt charts are a favored tool utilized in project scheduling and time administration. They visually represent the project timeline, illustrating the start and end dates of various tasks, their dependencies, and the overall progress. Each task is depicted as a horizontal bar spanning the planned duration, with its position and length indicating the task's timing and duration. Modifications in the length or position of these bars mirror shifts in task schedules. Gantt charts are vital for tracking project milestones and deadlines, comprehending the sequence of tasks, and visualizing the project's progress.

Earned Value Management (EVM): EVM is a project performance measurement methodology that amalgamates scope, cost, and time to assist the project manager in assessing and quantifying project performance and progress. It involves calculating three key metrics: the Planned Value (PV), which is the estimated cost for planned work; the Actual Cost (AC), which is the actual cost incurred for the work performed; and the Earned Value (EV), which is the value of the work actually completed. From these, performance indices such as Cost Performance Index (CPI) and Schedule Performance Index (SPI) can be calculated. If these indices are less than 1, it suggests that the project is over budget or behind schedule. Additionally, EVM can be utilized to forecast future performance and estimate at completion costs, providing valuable insights for decision-making.

Risk Register: A risk register, often referred to as a risk log, is an essential tool in project management. It acts as a central storage for all recognized project risks, with each risk logged alongside its attributes like its probability of occurrence, potential impact on the project if realized, risk category, and recommended mitigation or response strategies. The register enables structured risk analysis, risk prioritization, and tracking of risk management actions. Through frequent updating of the risk register, project managers can sustain a consistent and proactive approach to risk management, ensuring that all possible threats to the project's success are identified, understood, and suitably dealt with in a timely manner.

Change Control Systems: Change is unavoidable in projects, and it can influence various elements including scope, schedule, cost, and quality. Change control systems are formal procedures established to manage and control these changes. They assist in ensuring that any proposed change is thoroughly documented, evaluated for its potential impact on the project, and approved or rejected through an authorized process. The system retains a record of all changes, including the reasoning for the change, its approval status, and any actions taken in response. In doing so, change control systems assist in preventing scope creep, maintain project control, and ensure the project remains aligned with its objectives despite any changes.

Meetings and Reports: Regular meetings and reports hold a pivotal role in project monitoring and control. They are fundamental elements of the project's communication plan. Status meetings provide an opportunity for team members to discuss progress, exchange updates, highlight issues, and brainstorm solutions. They encourage teamwork, alignment, and collaboration. Conversely, project status reports offer a structured and consistent format for conveying critical project information to stakeholders. They may cover areas such as the project's progress against milestones, budget and schedule status, risk and issue updates, and any changes to the project. By facilitating transparency and open communication, regular meetings and reports help ensure everyone stays informed, engaged, and aligned with the project objectives.

Lessons Learned Database: A lessons learned database is a knowledge management instrument that stores experiences and insights gained from past projects. It encompasses both successful practices worth replicating and mistakes to evade. The lessons may cover various aspects of the project, from technical decisions and project management practices to stakeholder management and team collaboration. Before a project concludes, the team reflects on the project process and outcomes, documenting their insights in this database. This becomes a valuable resource for future projects, as it enables teams to leverage past experiences and continuous learning to enhance their project management practices, boost their efficiency, and avoid repeating the same mistakes.

Project Variances

Within the realm of project management, the term variance refers to a difference between the projected and actual performance of a project. Variances may manifest in numerous project aspects, such as time, cost, scope, and quality. Often, they signify challenges that demand attention. Here's the approach to handle them:

Identify the Variance: Spotting a variance in a project is the initial crucial phase towards its management and control. In the context of project management, a variance denotes a deviation from the planned or expected performance. This discrepancy can be identified by routinely tracking project activities and juxtaposing the actual results with the project blueprint. Utilities like Earned Value Management (EVM) can prove to be pivotal in this endeavor. EVM amalgamates measures of scope, timeline, and cost to gauge project performance and advancement, thus enabling the detection of any variance in these vital project facets. Swift identification of the variance facilitates immediate action and curtails the potential adverse impacts on the project.

Analyze the Variance: Once a variance has been spotted, an in-depth investigation is required to comprehend its origin. This stage may involve revisiting relevant project records, engaging in discussions or interviews with team members, scrutinizing project data, or conducting a root cause analysis. The aim is to determine why the project isn't adhering to the planned course. Grasping the underlying cause is the cornerstone to concocting an effective solution to address the variance.

Evaluate the Impact: After understanding why the variance has transpired, it's crucial to ascertain the potential or actual impact of the deviation on the project. The assessment should evaluate how the variance might influence the project's objectives, timeline, budget, quality, and deliverables. This evaluation will assist in comprehending the severity of the problem and prioritizing the necessary rectification measures. It's important to recognize that some variances may be minor and not significantly affect the project's outcome, while others may demand immediate attention to keep the project on track.

Develop a Response Plan: Based on the root cause analysis and impact assessment, the subsequent step is to devise a response plan to tackle the variance. This strategy might encompass corrective measures to steer the project back onto its intended course, preventive steps to hinder the variance from worsening, or, in some instances, adjusting the project blueprint to incorporate the change. The response plan should be relayed to all relevant stakeholders, and its execution should be meticulously managed and monitored. This method ensures that the project remains under control, notwithstanding any unforeseen circumstances or alterations.

Implement the Plan: Following the formulation of a response plan, the next phase involves its execution. The implementation process can comprise a myriad of tasks, contingent on the variance's nature and the plan's specifics. For instance, resources may necessitate reallocation, timelines might require adjustment, or project methodologies might demand modification. Robust communication is vital at this juncture to guarantee that all team members and stakeholders comprehend the modifications, the reasons behind them, and their implications on the project. Such transparency aids in keeping everyone coordinated and committed to the project's successful completion.

Monitor the Results: Implementing the plan isn't the final stage of variance management. It's essential to persistently monitor project parameters following the response plan's execution to evaluate its efficacy and confirm that the variance has been adequately addressed. Regular status updates, meetings, reviews, and tools like project dashboards and earned value management can facilitate this monitoring. If the plan isn't delivering the expected outcomes, additional analysis may be called for, and the plan may necessitate revisions.

Document the Variance: Documentation, a fundamental aspect of project management, is often neglected amidst addressing pressing issues. However, maintaining extensive records of all variances, their origins, the response strategies employed, and the outcomes can furnish invaluable insights for upcoming projects. This documentation acts as a historical record that can be referenced when similar issues emerge in future projects. It also contributes to the organization's knowledge repository, improving the capability to effectively manage and control projects. Detailed documentation can be incorporated into the project's "lessons learned" database, offering a crucial resource for continuous enhancement of project management practices.

Chapter Ten: Project Closure

The closure phase is an official indicator of a project's completion. It involves an exhaustive review to confirm that all project tasks are wrapped up, goals have been met, and deliverables have been transferred to the client or stakeholders. This confirmation is a critical element of the project lifecycle as it eliminates any uncertainty about the project's status and finalization. It includes an official seal of approval from the project manager and key stakeholders, affirming that all the work has been performed according to the project plan and that the project has reached its endpoint. This definitive closure helps define the project boundaries and gives a sense of achievement to the project team.

The project closure stage provides an ideal moment for a detailed performance appraisal. It involves comparing the actual project outcomes with the initial plans and goals concerning scope, budget, timeline, and quality. This review can underscore areas where the project excelled, where it encountered difficulties, and how effectively these difficulties were resolved. Performance assessment provides a clear overview of the project's victories and deficits, offering valuable insights that can aid in refining planning and execution in upcoming projects.

The culmination of a project implies that resources dedicated to that project - such as personnel, equipment, software, or funds - can be freed up and redirected towards other endeavors. This step is vital for maintaining efficient resource utilization within the organization. Project team members may be reassigned to new projects, equipment and tools can be employed elsewhere, and any leftover budget may be reallocated. It's a crucial step in project closure, ensuring that resources aren't left unused or squandered once the project is concluded.

One of the most enriching elements of project closure is the identification, recording, and distribution of 'lessons learned.' This involves a reflective overview of the project, where team members can discuss what worked well, what could have been better, and how such enhancements can be incorporated into future projects. The lessons learned can cover a range of topics from technical facets to team dynamics, project management techniques, or stakeholder engagement. By recording these insights, organizations can continually refine their project management practices, boost efficiency, mitigate risks, and increase the success rate of upcoming projects.

The finalization of a project presents a meaningful chance to honor the diligence and accomplishments of the project team. Recognizing team contributions can manifest in several ways - ranging from public commendations in gatherings, personalized notes of gratitude, award functions, to festive team gatherings. This act of acknowledging hard work not only lifts team spirit but also fosters a sense of unity and togetherness within the team. It engenders a sense of pride in team members for their contributions and nurtures a feeling of affiliation and loyalty towards the organization. By cultivating a positive and supportive work atmosphere, such recognition can substantially enhance employee satisfaction and retention.

A crucial element of the project closure phase is the formal transfer of the project's ultimate deliverables to the client or stakeholders. This isn't merely about handing over a product or service, but it involves making sure that the client is equipped with everything they need to fully utilize the deliverable. Depending on the nature of the project, this might include supplying user guides, documentation, training for users, or support for maintenance. The project team may also need to ensure that all agreements are finalized, and all project-related commitments have been met. A well-orchestrated and methodical handover can increase customer satisfaction and pave the way for potential future projects with the client.

After the successful finalization of a project, it's crucial to gather and store all project-related documents, records, and data. This includes project plans, timelines, budget details, risk registers, minutes of meetings, project reports, design documents, and even correspondence. This stored information serves as a vital resource for upcoming projects, providing invaluable insights into project planning and execution. It also helps maintain transparency and can be utilized for audit purposes or to resolve any disputes that might surface post-project finalization. Furthermore, storing project data contributes to the organization's institutional memory, enabling the preservation and transfer of knowledge within the organization.

Lessons Learned

In the realm of project management, executing a project evaluation and compiling knowledge gained is an imperative action during the final phase of any project.

Once a project is wrapped up, the project manager has the responsibility to set up a project review session - often dubbed as a project post-analysis, debrief, or retrospective. The purpose of this meeting is to thoroughly analyze and reflect on the project, scrutinizing its triumphs, hurdles, and the lessons learned. The session should include all central project team members, along with pertinent stakeholders. If deemed suitable, the customer or end-user might also be invited to provide valuable external viewpoints. By organizing this session, you establish an atmosphere that encourages introspection and mutual learning, thereby paving the way for continuous progress in project management.

A project review session demands sufficient preparation to ensure fruitful discussions. Collect all necessary project paperwork, such as the project blueprint, project reports, logs of risk and alterations, issue registers, and any other relevant data or correspondence. This documentary evidence offers a complete overview of the project's journey and acts as a key point of reference during discussions. Attendees should be urged to go over this paperwork before the session to ready their thoughts and contributions.

The session should kick off with a quick run-through of the project, recapping its goals, key milestones, broad timeline, final deliverables, and main results. This sets the stage for the subsequent conversation. Following this, the session dialogue should revolve around three main areas: what went right, what didn't hit the mark, and what could be enhanced for future projects. Fostering an open and sincere communication environment is critical during these talks, ensuring that the team grasps that the goal is learning and enhancement, not blaming or pointing fingers.

Initiate the discussion on an upbeat note by asking participants to share their thoughts on what worked well during the project. This might include areas like effective communication, successful problem-solving, efficient management of resources, punctual delivery, or innovative strategies that proved to be particularly effective. Also, consider acknowledging individual or team achievements that contributed to the project's success. Highlighting these successes not only lifts team spirits but also helps identify practices that could be repeated in future projects.

Stimulate team members to openly converse about any hurdles, complications, or setbacks they faced throughout the project. These issues may be tied to management of scope (for instance, scope creep), budget-related problems (like cost overruns), scheduling difficulties (such as missed deadlines), communication mishaps, or other process or quality complications. The motive behind this exercise isn't to lay blame, but to comprehend the problems encountered and pinpoint ways to circumvent similar complications in the future. By discussing these issues candidly, the team can build a common understanding of the obstacles that arose and the impacts they had on the project.

For each point discussed, the team should analyze how similar triumphs can be duplicated, or problems avoided, in the future. Aim for specific, actionable suggestions rather than generalized or unclear advice. For instance, instead of suggesting "we need better communication," you might recommend "we should organize weekly project status meetings to keep everyone updated."

Ensure that the lessons determined are recorded in a precise, succinct, and actionable format. Each lesson should include a description of what was learned, why it's significant, and how it can be applied to future projects. This record, typically known as a 'Lessons Learned Report', should be stored in a readily accessible location, like a centralized project management system or a shared document repository. This guarantees that it's conveniently available for reference when strategizing and executing future projects.

The value of lessons learned lies in their application to future projects. Commit to incorporating these lessons into the planning and execution of all future projects. This might involve revising your project management procedures, updating your project management tools, or offering additional training for your team. By implementing these lessons, you consistently enhance your project management strategies, and boost the chances of success in your future endeavors.

Celebrating Success

Celebration and acknowledgment are vital elements in maintaining a buoyant team spirit, fostering a positive work atmosphere, and fueling enthusiasm among team members. It's not merely about commemorating the completion of a project, but also about appreciating the effort, participation, and triumphs that transpired throughout its lifespan.

Valuing victories and appreciating the diligence of the team is extremely crucial in any project management setting. This transcends simply noting the conclusion of the project. By celebrating accomplishments and acknowledging effort, you give team members a sense of pride and satisfaction. They perceive their work as cherished and respected, which consequently elevates their spirits and motivation. Moreover, acknowledgment can also nurture a sense of responsibility and pride within team members, making them more dedicated to their tasks. It also promotes positive reinforcement, enabling individuals to link their efforts with recognition and appreciation. This is instrumental in crafting a conducive work environment, leading to improved productivity and job contentment. Such celebrations also offer a breather from the usual work routine, aiding in reducing stress and burnout.

While celebrating shared success is vital, it's equally important to value individual contributions. Each team member brings distinct skills and talents to the project, and their personal participation plays a significant role in the project's triumph. Acknowledging individual contributions can occur during team meetings or through private, one-on-one communication. It's vital to appreciate not just the major accomplishments, but also the smaller victories and efforts that might otherwise be overlooked. This could be someone working overtime to finish a task, finding an inventive solution to a complex problem, or going the extra mile to support a teammate. Acknowledging these efforts sends a message that every contribution, no matter how minor, is valued and contributes to the project's overall success.

While individual contributions are the building blocks of a project, the ultimate success is a group achievement. Therefore, it's crucial to celebrate team victories. These celebrations can be associated with significant project milestones or planned as a grand conclusion at the end of the project. The celebrations don't necessarily have to be grandiose or expensive. It could be a team lunch, an outdoor activity, or just a simple get-together with some snacks and refreshments. The main aim is to provide an environment where the team can gather to celebrate their joint achievement. This not only strengthens team cohesion but also conveys that their hard work and commitment have been recognized and appreciated. Such celebrations also offer a chance for the team to unwind and relax after a period of intense work, helping to reenergize them for future projects.

Cultivating an atmosphere of gratitude within a team is critical in fostering a collaborative and supportive working environment. Peer acknowledgment is an influential tool that not only drives individuals but also fortifies team relationships. When team members publicly recognize and appreciate each other's efforts, it instills a sense of belonging and camaraderie. Promoting peer acknowledgment can be facilitated through various techniques. For instance, a 'kudos' system can offer a platform for team members to publicize their appreciation for their colleagues' achievements, efforts, or helpful behavior. During routine team gatherings, allocate some time for peer-to-peer acknowledgment. This could be a dedicated session where team members get the chance to appreciate their colleagues' dedication, innovative concepts, or assistance. This practice of mutual acknowledgment emphasizes the value of every team member's contribution and can significantly improve team dynamics and spirit.

A structured acknowledgment program can be an extremely effective way to stimulate and reward your team. Such a program appreciates and rewards specific accomplishments, efforts, or behaviors that positively contribute to the project and align with the team's ideals and goals. The rewards in such a program don't necessarily need to be financial. They could take various forms, such as extra vacation time, gift vouchers, public acknowledgment during team gatherings, or opportunities to work on engaging projects or tasks. The key is to ensure the rewards are meaningful and valued by the team members. A well-conceived acknowledgment program not only motivates individuals but also sets the benchmark for what is considered extraordinary performance, thereby motivating others to strive for similar achievements.

While recognition at milestones is important, acknowledgment should not be limited to just significant accomplishments or the project's conclusion. Consistent recognition throughout the project lifecycle can play a pivotal role in sustaining team spirit high and maintaining motivation. This could be as simple as expressing appreciation when you see someone making an extra effort, or acknowledging a team member's progress during team gatherings. Making acknowledgment a regular practice communicates the message that every effort is significant, and that each team member's contribution is cherished. This not only enhances individual motivation but also fosters a positive work atmosphere where individuals feel noticed, valued, and appreciated for their efforts.

Conclusions and Recommendations

We live in an era of incessant change and progression, most notably in areas of technology and industry norms. This perpetual transformation is also mirrored in project management, a field where rising technologies, shifting project tendencies, advancing methodologies, and newly formulated regulatory prerequisites continually sculpt the terrain. In this light, perpetual learning becomes not just a choice, but an essential aspect for project managers. Through active participation in ongoing education and professional growth, project managers can remain abreast of the newest tools, comprehend and adjust to innovative methodologies, and keep up with modifications in industry regulations. This forms the cornerstone of staying pertinent, proficient, and effectual in their role. The capacity to promptly acclimate to new trends and transformations is vital not only for an individual project manager's career advancement but also directly affects the victory and effectiveness of the projects they manage.

Continuous learning paves the way for project managers to periodically refresh and broaden their skillsets, thereby intensifying their proficiency and effectiveness. It arms them with the knowledge to adeptly use new project management tools, adjust to freshly inducted methodologies, or adhere to updated regulatory prerequisites. Additionally, it allows project managers to draw insights from various industries and disciplines, fostering innovative thought and problem-solving capabilities. This elevated proficiency directly contributes to the overall triumph and quality of projects, enhancing the project manager's professional standing and career advancement.

Learning doesn't merely involve procuring new knowledge and skills, but it also pertains to reflecting on past experiences and deriving learning from them. Every project brings with it an abundance of lessons—stemming from both victories and setbacks. Reflective learning encompasses dissecting what was successful, what fell short, and what could be altered in future projects. This aids project managers in identifying areas for augmentation and formulate strategies for implementing modifications in future projects. This practice of reflective learning encourages a culture of continuous advancement and growth, leading to improved performance, heightened efficiency, and enhanced project outcomes over time.

In a dynamic corporate sphere, keeping up with the latest trends and technological advances can offer project managers a significant edge. As new instruments, techniques, and protocols surface, they often present prospects for enhancing efficiency and effectiveness in project execution. For example, rising technologies such as AI and machine learning can handle repetitive tasks, liberating project managers to concentrate on strategic decision-making. In a similar vein, comprehending and embracing the most recent project management techniques can aid in simplifying processes and improving project delivery. By exploiting these novel technologies and methodologies, project managers can introduce innovative strategies to their projects, enhancing project results and contributing to the overall triumph of their corporations.

Information is strength, a fact that holds particularly true in the domain of project management. The more a project manager learns and acquires experience, the more they bolster their self-assurance in their abilities. This confidence is not only about personal conviction; it directly impacts their professional abilities. A confident project manager is more resolute, making informed and efficient decisions that can guide a project towards successful culmination. They're also adept at managing and leading teams, as confidence often invokes trust and admiration from team members. This subsequently improves team productivity and cooperation. Therefore, the confidence derived from perpetual learning is an indispensable tool that significantly boosts a project manager's efficiency.

The arena of project management is competitive, and differentiating oneself often demands more than just foundational skills and experience. Continuous learning illustrates an enduring dedication to personal and professional growth, a characteristic greatly esteemed by employers. It equips project managers with a competitive edge over their colleagues. Be it achieving a new project management accreditation, learning to navigate a new project management software, or mastering a fresh methodology, each learning milestone augments a project manager's portfolio. These unending learning endeavors can pave the way to increased job prospects, elevated responsibilities, and career progression. Therefore, continuous learning is not only about maintaining relevance; it's a route to exhilarating career opportunities and advancement.

Apply what you have learned!

As we come to the end of our introductory journey into project management, it's vital to note that the insights garnered from this guide should not remain purely academic. Instead, they are designed to act as a launchpad for practical implementation in your professional path. Knowledge in a vacuum is static, but when utilized, it metamorphoses into a potent instrument that can mould projects, career trajectories, and even entire sectors.

The actual application of the principles, apparatus, and tactics elaborated in this guide is what truly animates them. At its core, project management is an exercise. It's not merely about comprehending methodologies, but about leveraging them to yield tangible, real-world outcomes.

Although the theoretical understanding procured from this guide offers a robust base, it's the hands-on application that genuinely vivifies project management principles. As you progress in your professional journey, perceive this knowledge not as a scholarly drill, but as a practical toolkit that you can use to steer your projects. You should strive to actively integrate the tactics, tools, and methodologies you've acquired into your project management practice. Keep in mind, project management isn't just about grasping the tenets; it's about utilizing them to produce measurable, real results. Every project you undertake offers a unique opportunity to employ what you've assimilated and transmute theoretical knowledge into practical proficiency.

Try, Experiment and Learn! One of the most effective learning methods is by execution. As you start applying the project management principles and techniques you've acquired, don't hesitate to experiment. Each project you manage is distinctive, encompassing its own set of goals, limitations, and stakeholders. This uniqueness implies that there's no uniform approach. Don't hesitate to try different methods and tools to identify what's most effective in a specific circumstance. Be receptive to making errors and learning from them. Each misstep provides invaluable insights that can assist you in honing your approach, thereby improving your project management skills over time.

Adapt and Customize! The methodologies and tools introduced in this guide are not inflexible rules but adaptable frameworks. Feel free to modify and tailor them to best meet your project's requirements and your work style. Whether it's fine-tuning a project management methodology to align better with your project's context or adjusting a tool to make it more convenient for your team, the key is to make the knowledge you've gained work for you. The ultimate aim is to devise a project management strategy that fits your unique circumstances and allows you and your team to efficiently deliver successful projects.

Share and Collaborate! Project management is a collective endeavor. As you amass more knowledge and experience, make sure to impart your learnings to your team members and stakeholders. Collaborative learning and knowledge sharing can cultivate a culture of ceaseless progress and innovation within your organization. It empowers others, motivating them to share their own insights and experiences, which can enhance the collective comprehension and performance of your team. Remember, the most triumphant project managers are not just those who excel at managing projects; they're also those who nurture growth and learning within their teams.

Apply Gradually! Given the breadth of data and the spectrum of methodologies and tactics presented in this guide, it's normal to feel a tad daunted. Don't let this dishearten you. Rather than attempting to implement everything simultaneously, start with small steps. Initiate by incorporating a technique or two into your ongoing projects and monitor the outcome. Note how these alterations influence your project's advancement and your team's output. As you grow more comfortable and assured with these techniques, slowly embed more of what you've absorbed into your project management practice. Each new tactic or methodology will broaden your capabilities and enhance your efficiency as a project manager.

Reflect and Learn! Contemplation is a potent instrument for learning and development. After every project, set aside time to reflect on what was effective, what wasn't, and what you could refine for the future. This reflective practice can garner valuable insights that directly feed into your evolution as a project manager. It cultivates a cycle of continuous learning, permitting your project management approach to adjust and progress in alignment with your expanding experience and the diverse nature of your projects. Always strive to glean something novel from each project, irrespective of its size or significance.

As we conclude this guide, it's my aspiration that the knowledge you've garnered will act as a sturdy basis for your expedition into project management. However, bear in mind that this is just the outset. Ongoing learning, advancement, and practical implementation are essential elements of your continuing journey. Project management goes beyond just accumulating knowledge; it's about converting that knowledge into action. It's about not just comprehending principles but applying them to yield successful projects.

Equipped with the knowledge you've acquired, you are now primed to dive deeper into the realm of project management. As you proceed, apply what you've learned and continue to pursue new knowledge. The authentic learning in project management, like many things in life, arises from action. Every new project is a chance to exercise your skills and gain invaluable experience. So, venture forward and embrace the dynamic, gratifying, and occasionally challenging world of project management. Remember, every move you make is a stride towards becoming a more proficient and triumphant project manager.

Good luck on your project management journey! I trust that the principles and practices discussed in this book will be a helpful guide as you navigate your path.

Printed in Great Britain
by Amazon

27018827R00088